CW00435316

Through the Blood and the Fire

*A Muslim fanatic becomes
a fiery evangelist
for Jesus Christ*

Christopher Alam

New Wine Press

New Wine Press
PO Box 17
Chichester
West Sussex PO20 6YB
England

All Bible quotations are from the Authorised Version.

ISBN 1 874367 28 0

Typeset by CRB (Drayton) Typesetting Services, Norwich
Printed in England by Clays Ltd, St Ives plc.

Contents

Foreword

I am always interested in reading about real people and about how they cope with life.

Christopher's story is exciting, challenging, and above all an inspiration for people who want to find the reality of God.

The accounts of Christopher's early life, unhappy childhood and his search for inner peace, and then his hideous persecution when he turned to Christianity make for lively and heartening reading.

Christopher's personal story is a classic one of conquering mountainous difficulties and hardships and coming out as a true warrior of the Gospel.

Pastor Ray McCauley
Rhema Bible Church
Randburg, South Africa

Introduction

Many people over the years, have asked me to put my story down in writing. I have been hesitant, as I want the focus of my ministry to be upon the Lord Jesus alone, and not upon myself, or any other man. However, a couple of years ago, I felt a clear leading in my heart to write this book, and so, here it is.

I want this book to be to the Glory of God, that it would help many to find the living and true Jesus Christ, and also be an encouragement to many.

I want to thank God for my precious wife Britta, who stands faithfully by my side, and has always encouraged and put up with me.

I want to acknowledge the role that men like Kenneth E. Hagin, Reinhard Bonnke and Ray McCauley have played in my life. Also my pastor Sam Smucker, and many others who have touched and influenced me positively through the years.

Special thanks to my co-labourers working alongside me in Dynamis Världsevangelisation. Together we have stood and seen God's Fire fall and change multitudes of lives.

All Glory be to God.

Christopher Alam

Chapter 1

He Gives us a Sign

It was a warm, sunny day. Thousands of people packed the stands at the soccer stadium. This was Blagoevgrad, a town of about 100,000, in the part of biblical Macedonia that today is part of Bulgaria. I was preaching a simple gospel message about Jesus, with all the faith and passion in my heart. Right in the middle of my message, preaching about the death of Jesus upon Calvary's Cross, His Resurrection, Ascension, and coming Return, I cried out, **'Jesus is coming back! Are you ready to meet Him? Are you ready?'** Suddenly the Power of God exploded over the stadium. It happened all at once. Thousands of people began jumping down off the stands, onto the field, and ran towards the platform. Hands in the air, voices crying out to God for His mercy, tears running down their cheeks, they knelt or stood, a sea of humanity crowding the field in front of the platform. I found myself at a total loss for words. Right in the middle of a fiery salvation message, the Holy Spirit had just moved in and taken over the place. What can a man preach, or do, or say at such a moment?

Tears came to my eyes, my voice choked over. I just could not say anything any more. I gave the microphone to Pastor Milcho Totev, a Bulgarian pastor, and mumbled to him to lead the crowd in the prayer for salvation.

Totally overwhelmed by God's presence and power, I went to the rear part of the platform, knelt behind some chairs, and just wept. The glory of God was sweeping all over the stadium as thousands received Jesus, the Son of God, as their Lord and Saviour.

'Thank you, Lord Jesus!' was all I could say, 'thank you for saving me when I was so low down, thank you for bringing me so far, and for letting me see your power and your glory! You have brought me such a long way, dear Jesus. Thank you Lord!'

Later during the service the Lord graciously confirmed His Word with signs, wonders and miracles. The hopelessly crippled walked, the blind saw, deaf ears were opened, proving to this former stronghold of communism, that Jesus Christ truly is the same today as He was 2000 years ago.

'Thank you Jesus!' was all I could say as I knelt and wept.

That night in my hotel room, I just lay there thanking and praising God, who is so gracious and merciful that he could love a once-hopeless case like me, cleanse me, make me a new person, and use me in His service, for His glory.

Chapter 2

Muslim Roots

I was born on the 29th of March 1954 in a Muslim home in Pakistan. My ancestors, on my father's side of the family, were Hashemite Arabs. We were 'Syeds', directly descended from Mohammad, the founder of Islam. Mohammad had only one son, Ibrahim, who died in infancy; consequently, the family line runs through his daughter Fatima, who became the wife of Ali. My uncle had in his possession a copy of of our family tree, tracing our family lineage all the way back to Mohammad (from Mohammad, one can trace the family line backwards through Ishmael to Abraham). My grandfather was a very religious man, having made the pilgrimage to Mecca. He had been decorated by the British government for his services to the Empire.

My father, as I recall him in my early years, was not a totally religious person. I remember him facing Mecca and praying to Allah every evening. After that he and my mother would then go off to the Officers' Club or some nightclub in the city, often coming back drunk very late at night. We always had sizeable stocks of liquor at home, yet we often hosted all-night 'milad shareefs' (prayer-cum-Quran recital meetings) and other religious gatherings in our home. Later on, as the years went by, my father and became very religious, even making a number of pilgrimages to Mecca.

My father engaged religious tutors who came to our home and taught me to read the Quran in the original Arabic. I memorized several chapters and verses from the Quran, and could recite them, yet without understanding what I was saying. We never spoke or understood Arabic (except for a few words and phrases), yet we read the Quran in Arabic. This was because Muslims consider Arabic a holy language, being Mohammad's mother language, and there is thus supposed to be special merit and blessing in reading the Quran in Arabic. This is why many Muslims can claim that they have read the Quran, but they have never really understood it, never having learnt old classical Arabic.

The Pakistani religious environment I grew up in was wholly and totally Muslim. I had no knowledge of the beliefs of Christianity or other religions. I, like everybody else, believed that Islam was the only way to God. 'There is no god but Allah, and Mohammad is his prophet', as the Muslim creed or confession of faith states.

We used to visit the tombs of Muslim saints, where we would pray, asking for Allah's favour. My father was a devotee of a number of 'pirs' (Muslim mystics and 'holy men'). I often accompanied him when he visited them. Some of them acted really strange, and some used to say some really weird things. We held these men in awe, and the thought of ever questioning their credibility never once crossed our minds. I concluded that what I took to be their oddness and weirdness was actually signs of them being really close to Allah. After all, this is what mysticism really was all about!

I remember one such 'holy man' with magical powers who visited our home. He was Hazrat Bahawal Shah from a village outside the city of Sahiwal, and was reputed to be 125 years old. My father had brought him in to pray for our family, and to bless us. The old man ordered a kerosene stove to be brought in. The stove was brought in, put on the floor, and lit. A large pan of oil was then put on the stove. The oil was heated up until it began to boil. Then I, as the eldest son in the family, was told to put my foot into the boiling oil! I had no choice but to obey. The old man began chanting something in Arabic. I plunged my foot into the boiling oil ... it felt like lukewarm bathwater! I did not get burnt at all.

Another 'holy man' broke off a leaf of a creeping plant, swung his arm around, and lo! it turned it into a large sugar crystal! This, and other such experiences further affirmed our faith in Allah.

Today I can see that all this was witchcraft, but in those days things such as these would hold me in awe. One thing I understand today is that demonic powers are real, but the power of God is much stronger. Demonic power can be outwardly spectacular and impressive, but it never adds anything to a person's life; in fact, people who have been touched by such demonic power soon begin to sense oppression in the soulish realm of their lives. Many even develop serious physical or psychosomatic illnesses. The power of God, on the other hand, brings restoration, healing, assurance, love, joy and peace to the one who experiences it.

Socially, we belonged to the upper class. We had servants who waited on us day and night. We often had parties and dinners in our home. In fact, our home was a sort of 'gathering point' for military officers, friends and relatives. We always ate well. Meat was on our table every day. Hot breakfasts, multi-course lunches and multi-course dinners were normal, everyday fare. Pakistani food is usually very strongly spiced with hot chillies, but my father never really could handle hot spices. A result of this was that our food at home, though delicious, was never very strongly spiced. Because of this I never really learnt to handle strongly spiced food either.

I grew up speaking three languages, English with my father, Bengali with my mother, and Urdu with our servants. After some years, a fourth language, Punjabi, was also introduced into our household. These four languages were in everyday use in our family.

My mother was a very talented woman. In those days, before television came to Pakistan, everyone listened to the radio. My mother read the news over the radio. She was also a singer, and was often invited to sing at musical soirées and concerts.

I went to the best schools. These were schools run by Roman Catholic nuns, mostly Irish. There were quite a number of these schools, and they were considered the best academically. I remember that over the blackboard in every classroom there hung a crucifix with the figure of a man crucified on it. He seemed to be looking down at us from the cross upon which he hung. On the back wall behind me was a portrait of a man wearing a crown of thorns. Blood trickled down from his brow and he had a purple coloured heart. All the years I went to those schools, nobody ever told me who this man was, and why he hung upon the cross. Although just a boy, I often wondered but never asked, and nobody ever told me either.

My father was an officer in the Pakistan Army. A graduate of the Indian Military Academy in Dehra Dun, India (The 'Sandhurst' or 'West Point' of India). He was trained by the British when they still ruled the region that today is known as India and Pakistan. An artillery officer, he also served some years as commanding officer for the East Pakistan section of the famous ISI (Inter Services Intelligence). He was decorated for gallantry under fire during some covert operation he was engaged in while with the ISI. I was proud of my father. We always lived in military cantonments, except the years he served in the ISI and we lived in town, in a civilian area. During that time he always wore civilian clothes, and we were told never to reveal his military identity to anyone. I was to tell people that he was a businessman. We had strange 'uncles' who always visited us, and there was always a lot of 'cloak and dagger' activity around us. Everything was 'hush-hush'.

I grew up with the military, I loved the uniforms, the soul-stirring skirl of bagpipes, the smell of cordite in the firing ranges. I had decided that one day I too, would wear the khaki uniform my father wore with such pride. He rose to a very high rank in the Pakistan Army. My father, uncle and three cousins rose to general ranks in the armies of Pakistan and Bangladesh. At the time of writing two uncles are ministers in the government, and my mother is a member of parliament in Bangladesh. We socialized with the top people. Among our family friends was the late General Zia-ul-Haq, President of Pakistan until his aircraft was blown out of the sky some years ago.

This is the kind of background I come from.

My early childhood was very happy, but in 1962, my parents got divorced. Because I was only eight years old, and divorce was a very rare thing in Pakistan, I did not understand what had happened. My father was stationed at Dhaka, now the capital of Bangladesh. We went to see my mother off at the railway station. As the train left, my little brother and I stood on the platform waving her goodbye. We thought that she would be back in a few days, that she was merely visiting her mother. Little did we know that she would never come back to us.

My father remarried soon after. My little brother who was four years younger than me, and I were told that this lady was our 'new mother'. Little did I realize how drastically she would influence my existence.

My stepmother was a very cruel woman. She was very pleasant in the beginning, but after some time she began to beat my brother and me. The violence grew in intensity as time passed. I was beaten almost daily. As days turned into months and years, the physical and emotional torture increased. I was beaten often, and for little or no reason. She was always nice when my father was around, but when he was away, she became a different person. She would grit her teeth in rage until I could hear sounds like bones cracking.

I eventually plucked up enough courage to tell my father what was happening. His answer was a resounding slap on my face. He shouted at me, hit me, and called me a liar. That day I felt that I had lost my father too.

My life had become a nightmare. I began to read lots of fairy tales and found that the beautiful world of fairy tales was one I could escape to, away from reality, to find solace and comfort. I would often cry myself to sleep. This went on for a few years. Life became unbearable, and I began to lose my desire to live. I became withdrawn, afraid, insecure and morose.

I had lost my childhood.

Christopher (right) with his half brother

A 16 year old cadet at Pakistan Air Force College in Sargodha

Christopher Alam at Pakistan Air Force College (circled)

Chapter 3

Air Force College

In 1967, just as I turned 13, I applied for enrolment in the Pakistan Air Force College, and after all kinds of tests, was accepted as a Cadet. I spent five years, from the age of 13 to 18, in the Air Force College. These five years set their stamp upon my life.

Several hundred of us lived together in a closed environment, right next to the large Air Force Base at Sargodha. We were close to the end of the main runway, and quickly became used to the sounds of different kinds of aircraft taking off and landing day and night. We could soon tell the different kinds of aircraft by their engine noise. We slept in dormitories with 16 beds. Winters were very cold and frosty, and temperatures were close to freezing. We had no heating or running hot water. Washing and showering in the ice-cold winters was quite an experience! As the cold water hit our bodies, we would sing at the top of our lungs, to try to make the ice-cold water more bearable!

For the cadets, life consisted of studies, drills, parades, sports, hard physical exertion, and inspections, etc. There were many sports fields and open spaces in the College grounds. We played soccer, basketball, field hockey, cricket or athletics every evening. Discipline was hard, and physical punishment was meted out for all kinds of reasons, big and small. These punishment sessions were called 'Extra Drills', and were 45 minutes long. Extra Drills were held under the afternoon sun, with temperatures rising to 110°F–120°F in the summer. We had to run around with heavy old .303″ Lee-Enfield No.1 rifles raised above our heads, 'at the double' or 'frog jumping', that is, squatting on the ground and hopping forwards like a frog.

We all aspired to be fighter pilots in the Air Force. Our heroes were fighter pilots, past graduates of the college, who would often come to visit their old alma mater. They were billeted in the Air Force Officers' Mess. I remember one pilot, a Flight Lieutenant, who visited us one evening. He was our number one idol. That evening he sipped tea and relaxed with some of us, wearing his flying suit. The next morning we were told that he had crashed and died soon after he had visited us. His Mirage-III fighter-interceptor had hit the ground as he was flying low at treetop-level. This put us all of us in a sombre mood. I saw when they brought in his remains in a flag-draped coffin, stood at attention, and saluted. This incident jarred everybody and reminded us of the frailty of human existence; that we all are only a heart-beat away from eternity.

Every day started with parade, inspection, saluting the flag, and a reading from the Koran. We were indoctrinated and taught about Islam. Fasting during the month of Ramadhan was compulsory. We ate a huge meal at 3 am every morning, and then fasted until just after sunset, all the while working in the heat of the day without letting a drop of water touch our lips. The fast was very strict. Even swallowing our own saliva could break the fast. This was supposed to purify us spiritually, but we seemed to remain the same old sinners we had always been. Friday prayers in the mosque were also compulsory. Some of us were very religious and prayed five times a day in the mosque, every single day.

I had thought that getting away from my parents would solve all my problems. But sadly, the beatings, the emotional and physical torture I had endured since the age of eight, had left deep emotional scars. No matter how hard I tried, the past followed me like my shadow, and I had deep problems. It affected me academically, and my general performance was affected so adversely that I was sent for psychological tests and evaluation.

Although they found me to be of normal intelligence, nobody really understood why I was always at the bottom of my class. Before the High School Board examinations, while I was visiting my father, he told me how worthless I was, and that the only reason I still was his son was because 'it was so, legally'. He threatened to disown me if I did not do well in the examination, as my failure would bring shame and disgrace to his name.

This hurt me, and I decided to 'show him that I was as good as anyone else' in the exams. I crammed for the examination as one possessed, passing with excellent grades. My father showed no sign of appreciation. The only thing he said was that he was ashamed of me because the son of a friend of his had done much better than I had in the same examination! This hurt terribly, and I felt that no matter how hard I tried, I just wasn't good enough. Why should I even try? Everybody else saw my good grades as some kind of divine intervention! After these exams, I was down again, at the bottom of my class. Nobody encouraged me. I saw myself as a born loser, a total failure, and felt that I had no reason to live. My grades were so bad that one of my instructors wrote very plainly on my annual report card, 'He is hopeless. Only Allah can help him!'

In 1971 trouble started brewing in the eastern province of Pakistan, now callèd Bangladesh, and everybody anticipated war with India. I had come to a point where my life was one of total despair. I did not want to live anymore. Suicidal thoughts obsessed my mind. I was very aware that I was a sinner, and would go to hell. Very aware of the reality of heaven and of hell, I was afraid to go to hell, and the fear of hell was basically what kept me alive. However, we had been taught that a sinful Muslim would go to heaven if he fell in battle in 'jihad', or a 'holy war'. Knowing that war against India was always a 'holy war', I began to prepare myself. I fasted, prayed, spent hours in the mosque reading the Koran. At times I was even entrusted with calling out the 'azan', the Muslim call for prayer that is heard from minarets. I wept before Allah, pleading with him to grant me martyrdom in the coming war against India.

Just before the war started, we worked very hard at the Air Base, digging trenches and filling sand-bags. After this, all cadets were dispersed and sent home. I was sent to Lahore, where my father was commanding an artillery brigade. The war started in December 1971. I tried desperately to get to the front-lines, where I could join the battle, but I was stopped by an army Field Intelligence Unit, who were surprised to see me making my way to the front in Air Force uniform. The closest I got to the battle was at the artillery command post. In the distance I could see thousands of muzzle flashes of the big 155 mm guns lighting up the cold December night, and hear the sounds of the battle raging in the distance. I did my best to get into the thick of it, but it just didn't work.

I helped with the war effort as much as I could, trying to get into the action. Low-level air raids were an everyday occurence, and when the enemy aircraft came in, they not only attacked their targets, but also any source of anti-aircraft fire. With this in mind, I got on a rooftop with a rifle during an air raid, ready to open fire. Everybody was so terrified that they dragged me off the roof. I wanted so desperately to die, because martyrdom in a 'holy war' would open the doors of heaven for me.

I was 17 years old, and my greatest desire was to die.

Chapter 4

The Aftermath of War

The war, bloody and furious, lasted only a short while. Pakistani forces in East Pakistan surrendered, resulting in East Pakistan becoming the independent nation of Bangladesh. The United Nations stepped in and negotiated a cease-fire in West Pakistan, where we were.

Thousands of young men died, and large numbers were maimed or crippled for life. I visited the military hospital, overflowing with wounded. The things that I saw would turn the stomachs of the most hardened.

I knew a lieutenant, fresh out of the School of Infantry and Tactics. As he was on his way to join his battalion, his jeep ran over an anti-tank mine. Half his foot was blown off, but his driver and a soldier with them had been blown to bits. Another officer had half his leg blown off as he bravely led an attack across a minefield. He screamed and moaned in pain day and night.

One major was lucky. A bullet had entered through his mouth, taking his front teeth, and passed through his neck, narrowly missing his spine. His whole company had been wiped out under a massive enemy attack with armoured support. Most of his men had been shell-shocked and had drowned in the knee-deep waters of the Sutlej river as they were retreating. I remembered when this had happened, because I was in the artillery command-post at that time. This officer had pleaded for artillery fire-support during the massive enemy attack, but it had not helped. After his company had been wiped out, and the the large enemy force had occupied the position and were digging-in, my father had ordered down such massive and concentrated artillery fire, that the enemy troops and armour had been literally blown to bits and decimated. I was there when it happened, following the radio-communications during the battle, and had seen the massive artillery barrage that followed.

I saw the **realities** of war. War is, at times, neccessary to preserve freedom when a country is under the threat of aggression, but it is basically evil, the consequence of man's sin, hate and greed. The 'glorified' image of war that movies present has no resemblance to the horrible reality of real war.

Pakistan lost the war, and 90,000 of our men were held prisoners of war by India, all captured at the surrender of Bangladesh to the Indian Army. One of my instructors from the Air Force College was among them. The whole nation was in a state of utter shock. If Allah was with us, a Muslim nation, how could we lose a war to the idol-worshippers of India? My faith and confidence in Allah were deeply shaken. It seemed like all I had so fanatically believed in didn't really amount to much in reality. I found myself becoming a confused agnostic, not really knowing what I believed anymore.

Chapter 5

Without Direction

The summer of 1972 marked the end of five years at the Air Force College. Just prior to then, my whole class went through the Inter-Services Selection Board tests in the military cantonment of Kohat. Most of us passed the four intensive days of physical and psychological tests we were put through. We were now cleared for two and a half years of training at the Pakistan Air Force Academy in Lower Topa and Risalpur, after which we would be full-fledged pilots in the Pakistan Air Force. All that remained now was the Intermediate College Examinations.

I was disillusioned, hurting and confused. I lacked motivation and failed the' exams. Most of my class-mates who passed went on to the Pakistan Air Force Academy, and some joined the army's Pakistan Military Academy in Kakul. The first thing I did was spend a month with an infantry battalion in Leepa Valley, in the mountains of Kashmir, one of the most beautiful places I have ever been to.

Not having definite plans for my future, I tried different things, but without any sense of direction. I found the adjustment to civilian life difficult. I worked for a while at an advertising agency as a copywriter/creative executive. After that I went back to college, to clear the examinations that I had failed at the Air Force College. I studied military science, passing by the skin of my teeth, but not before finding out which professors that would be checking the exam papers, and taking care to bribe them properly! At college I joined the Pakistan National Guards and did well, passing out as the best all-round cadet, and best marksman. I thus became a reserve officer in the Pakistan National Guards. This was, in a nutshell, a good picture of the paradox of my life so far. I did well at things that didn't really matter, but was a failure at the things that did matter and were important for my future. That was the sad truth about me.

By now my life was even more confused. I lived a life of sin and immorality, living on the brink of suicide. The army selected me for regular officers' training, but I felt that something within me just would not allow me to sign the papers. People thought that I was mad, as I was among only four selected out of a batch of 150 candidates, but I just did not feel that it was the right thing to do. So, giving no reason at all, I turned it down. I felt like getting away from everything. I was confused. My life was spiralling downwards. I knew that I would soon hit bottom and end my life. I was losing my grip on life itself.

I had some friends who belonged to the 'ahmadiyya' sect of Islam. Ordinary Muslims do not accept this group, as they believe in a 'prophet' or 'messiah', Mirza Ghulam Ahmed, who lived in the 1800s. Ordinary Muslims, on the other hand, believe that Mohammed was the last prophet, greater than and superceding all other prophets, and that there is no prophet after Mohammad. The 'ahmadiyya' seemed to be good, people. I joined the 'ahmadiyya', but soon realized that they did not have the answer that I was looking for. They may have been better people than most, but they could not heal a broken heart or give peace to a sinner.

As a last resort, I began to study to be a Radio Officer in the Merchant Marine. The idea was that going to sea, making lots of money and leaving my roots behind, would mean freedom, and would give me the peace I so longed for.

I had effectively left home when I was 13 and had never had a real childhood. Hurt and rejection had almost destroyed me. I had no real friends and was afraid of people. I stuttered and stammered when I was nervous, which was most of the time. Hatred towards my father, my stepmother and family was by now, rooted deep in my soul.

My younger brother attemped suicide. He lay there as we all stood shocked, waiting for the ambulance, while my stepmother screamed and cursed his unconscious form. He had left a note saying, among other things, that he was tired of all the beatings. My father came home and did not say a word; not a word of remorse. He seethed in tight-lipped fury that now outsiders would find out that our outwardly harmonious family 'had problems'.

I had not received a mother's love, having met her only a couple of times since the divorce. I did not love anyone, and nobody seemed to love me or see anything good in me. In fact I did not know how to receive love, or to give love. My memories of my lost childhood haunted and tormented me continually, and I just couldn't be free from them in order to live a normal life. It seemed that all I had gone through, all the hurtful words spoken over me, were what I had finally become.

I was almost 22 years old, and had nothing to live for.

Chapter 6

Strange Encounter

On a sunny day in December 1975 I was walking down Mall Road, the main thoroughfare of Lahore, Pakistan. Thousands of people were on the streets. Suddenly, among all the brown-skinned faces of my countrymen, I noticed a very tall white man. He was smiling broadly as he handed out what appeared to be sheets of printed paper to the crowd. I felt strangely drawn towards him. He smiled at me and gave me some of the literature that he was handing out to everybody.

'Who are you?' I asked him.

'I am a servant of Jesus Christ' he replied. 'I am from England, and travel all around the world, telling people about Jesus Christ.'

None of this made any sense to me. All I knew about Jesus Christ was that he was the prophet of the Christians, and the founder of Christianity, as we had Mohammad, the prophet of Islam. I had read in *Time* magazine about the new US president Jimmy Carter having said 'I am Born-Again!' I did not know what he meant, but it seemed to have something to do with the Christian religion. I had never met a born-again Christian, never met a preacher, and had never been inside a church. I had never even seen a Bible. I did not have the foggiest notion about what Christians believed in. All I knew was that Christians existed, and that just as all Pakistanis were Muslims, so were all white people Christians. As far as I knew, Adolf Hitler, Brigitte Bardot, James Bond, Mickey Mouse, and Marilyn Monroe were all Christians!

I left this smiling Englishman and continued on my way. A couple of hundred yards further, I had an indescribable urge to go back to him. It is hard to explain, but it was as if a physical force kept me from taking a step further. I just had to go back to him. I turned around and walked back to where he stood. I suddenly found myself pouring out my heart and telling him, a complete stranger, of all my hurts, pains, and longings. He listened, and then said, '**Jesus** can set you free!'

This sounded very strange to me, as I had been told that the prophet 'Isa', as we Muslims knew Jesus, had lived and been gone for thousands of years, and yet this man seemed to be saying that this Jesus was real and alive, today, and could turn my situation around now! I asked him how Jesus could do this.

'It's very simple' he said, 'All you have to do is to ask Him to come into your heart.'

All this was very strange and new to me, but something about this Jesus seemed to grip my soul. There seemed to be something powerful to the name 'Jesus' every time he spoke it. I had just tried about everything else, so why not give Jesus a chance too?

The Englishman took me aside and right there, in front of a BATA shoe shop and a pharmacy, he said, 'Okay now, let's pray together. Bow your head, close your eyes, and say this after me ...'

I did as he told me to, and repeated the words, '**Jesus**, come into my heart, and set me free. Thank you Jesus. Amen.'

I opened my eyes. Something felt different. I couldn't tell what it was, but I felt lighter inside, as though a burden had been removed from inside me, and a little spring had begun to bubble instead. I felt different.

'Let's meet at the YMCA tomorrow, at 10 am,' the Englishman said as I left.

(I never met this Englishman again. All he told me was that his name was 'Samson'. Many years later I did some detective work and found out that his real name was Keith Frampton, the son of the late Mr K.P. Frampton, of Bromley, England. Mr Frampton was a prominent Christian businessman with a great heart for God. He was a great supporter of missionary endeavours until his passing away to his heavenly reward a few years ago. I had the privilege of staying in the Frampton home and enjoying their hospitality and fellowship shortly before Mr Frampton's passing away a few years ago.)

Chapter 7

Changed from Within

As I went back home, I felt different. That evening one of the friends I that I used to 'walk on the wild side' with, suggested that we go out and have 'a good time.' I refused.

'What's wrong with you?' he asked.

'Nothing,' I said, 'but I can't do all this stuff with you anymore. You see, I have Jesus living in my heart!' These words just came out of my mouth, without me realizing what I was saying. My friend went hysterical.

'You mean you've become a Christian?' he yelled.

'Honestly, I don't know. All I know is that Jesus lives in my heart, and that He has set me free!'

My friend thought that I had gone mad.

'You can't do this! We are Muslims!' he shouted at me.

He argued hysterically for some time, and finally left. He wrote a long letter to my father who was stationed in Multan, a city about six hours drive to the south.

That evening I walked the streets, praising Jesus for the first time in my life. I had found a wonderful Saviour. I did not understand the fullness of what He done for me. I did not know about His death on the cross for me, or that He was risen. All I knew was that He had come into my heart. He had set me free, given me peace and joy, and I felt like a new man. I walked till late that night, singing to Jesus songs of worship and praise, songs I made up as I walked. Wave after wave of praise and worship poured out of the depths of my being to this Wonderful **Jesus**!

Chapter 8

A New Beginning

I went to the YMCA the next day to keep my appointment with the Englishman. I waited all day, but he never turned up. I waited the day after that with the same results. I went back the third day but he did not turn up that day either. During those three days I had undergone an awesome transformation. I was changed, a new person.

As I waited for the Englishman the third day, I saw a young man and woman come in, carrying the same kind of literature that the Englishman had given me. I approached them and asked about the Englishman. They said that he had to leave the country a couple of days earlier because of an emergency.

I told them what had happened to me. The young man, an American, put his Bible on my knee, and opened it. He put his finger on a certain passage and asked me to read. This was the first time in my life that I ever saw a Bible. The words I read said:

> *'Then said Jesus unto his disciples, If any man will come after me, let him deny himself, and take up his cross, and follow me. For whosoever will save his life shall lose it: and whosoever will lose his life for my sake shall find it. For what is a*

*man profited, if he shall gain the whole world,
and lose his own soul? or what shall a man give
in exchange for his soul?'*   (Matthew 16:24-26)

These words of Jesus struck me at the very depth
of my being, and at that moment I decided to follow
Jesus totally, wholly and at any cost. In a few minutes I was out on the streets with these foreigners,
handing out tracts, telling people the little I knew
about Jesus, 'He will set you free if you ask Him into
your heart!'

It was then that I sensed God calling me to serve
Him the rest of my life, by telling people about
Jesus.

The young American gave me a pocket New Testament and took me home for a meal. I found a
whole group of these young followers of Jesus,
singles, couples, and children. They told me that
they were from a group called 'The Children of
God'. Today, unfortunately, they are no more than a
false cult, but in those days I saw nothing that made
me doubt that they were anything other than genu-
ine Christians. A little girl sang for me, playing her
guitar. They showered me with such love that I was
completely overwhelmed. Never in my life had I
been treated with such love.

That night I went to bed crying, I cried tears of joy
at the love the Christians had shown me.

I was 22, but I felt like I had become a child all
over again.

Chapter 9

Fiery Persecution

The next day my father flew in from Multan, where he lived. He had received my friend's letter, and had taken the first available flight into Lahore.

All these years, he had cared so little; now, all of a sudden, he appeared to be very concerned. For a Muslim to leave Islam and follow Jesus has its consequences:

According to Islamic law, leaving Islam and becoming a Christian is punishable by death. The convert to Christ should thus be executed. In the Muslim world there are very few Muslims who become Christians and confess their faith openly. This is because they are usually killed by their own families. Very few, like me, survive, but most have to make the ultimate sacrifice for their faith in Jesus, laying down their lives. The police and authorities normally just look the other way. It is considered an act of virtue to kill an 'apostate' from Islam.

When a Muslim turns to Jesus, it is looked on as a great disgrace for the entire family. It is a stigma on the name and honour of the family. In the Muslim world, it is very important to maintain the family's pride in the eyes of society. The family therefore will try to get the new Christian to return to Islam. This is done firstly through offers of money and material things, and then through threats. If this doesn't work, the only way of salvaging the family pride and honour is by obeying the injunction of the Koran, to kill the new believer.

My father was furious. He got together some of his friends, a Major General, a Lieutenant-Colonel and a Major. They grilled me, insulted me, and called me all kinds of names. I had great peace in my heart, and took it all in my stride. This angered them even more. For two or three days they analysed me and finally came to the unanimous decision that I had been hypnotised and had gone completely mad!

I was admitted to the psychiatric ward of the Military Hospital in Lahore. The place was like a cage, guarded by uniformed soldiers carrying staves for protection from the crazy people locked up inside.

Some of the patients who were locked up there were really sick, but others were there for silly reasons. One man was there for refusing to salute a General! Another was one of the thousands of street beggars of Pakistan, but what made him special was that he was suspected of being a secret agent spying for Indian Intelligence! A situation like this was perfectly normal, considering the fact that we Pakistanis have always had a national mass-paranoia about India. A third man, an Air-Force sergeant, was there because he had stopped believing in Allah and had become an atheist!

I was given five different kinds of pills and capsules three times a day. The pills made me dizzy. I had smuggled in my little New Testament, but I could read no more than three verses at a time. I'd become giddy if I tried to read more. Nevertheless, the Word of God sustained me. During my two weeks in the place I led two people to the Lord Jesus, one was the atheist Air-Force Sergeant, the other was a male psychiatric nurse, a Medical Corps sergeant who was assigned to watch over us. He took me out of the 'cage' into the garden, and said, 'There is nothing wrong with you. Why are you here?'

I then proceeded to tell him about the Lord Jesus, and he prayed together with me to receive the Lord Jesus.

The doctor in charge of the ward had had enough of me and discharged me. Both he and I were glad to part company!

All this was just the beginning. My father took me to his 'pir', a supposedly 'holy man'. This old man cursed me, but he died some months later. After this I was taken to Multan and kept under guard in my father's house, surrounded by very high walls, and guarded by soldiers around the clock. Then a very interesting incident took place.

We knew a particular 'holy man' who had a lot of contact with the spirit world. He was in constant communication with 'djinns', what Christians would identify as evil spirits. We knew and had seen manifestations of supernatural activity around this man. He could call on these spirits to do things for him. He could put very strong curses on people, moving and influencing things through the demon spirits he moved with. This man was called in to work on me. For several days and nights he was in the bedroom next to mine, praying, saying incantations and mumbo-jumbo. Finally, he called me in and said, 'I believe you are doing the right thing.'

I was shocked!

He continued, 'I'll tell your father to leave you alone. You are doing the right thing. If you are wrong, you'll come back.'

The power of Jesus is greater than the power of the devil, and even the devil recognises and acknowledges it!

I managed to escape a few days later, travelling by bus to Lahore to join the 'Children of God' through whom I had received the Lord Jesus. All I had was about 7 rupees, equivalent to less than a dollar, a couple of changes of clothing, a toothbrush, a blanket, and a few other small things.

My father immediately set the police and the army looking for me. I slept in a different place every night to make it difficult for them to catch me. The Lord strengthened my heart through the 27th Psalm:

> *'The Lord is my light and my salvation; whom shall I fear? the Lord is the strength of my life; of whom shall I be afraid? ... One thing have I desired of the Lord, that will I seek after; that I may dwell in the house of the Lord all the days of my life, to behold the beauty of the Lord, and to inquire in his temple ... when my father and my mother forsake me, then the Lord will take me up ...'*

The Lord encouraged and strengthened me. I spent about a month in Lahore. I read the Bible, prayed and testified about Jesus every day. During those days that I received the greatest revelation of my life. It happened as I was reading my Bible, and found myself in the 53rd chapter of the Book of Isaiah.

'For he shall grow up before Him as a tender plant, and as a root out of a dry ground ... He is despised and rejected of men...'

Jesus was identifying himself with me!...

'Surely he hath borne our griefs, and carried our sorrows: ... But he was wounded for our transgressions, he was bruised for our iniquities: the chastisement of our peace was upon Him, and with His stripes we are healed.'

Suddenly the message of the Cross struck home! I saw it! I saw the Cross, the very crux of the Good News about Jesus! I now understood how **Jesus** actually **bore** upon Himself our sins and our torments upon Calvary's Cross.

I wept profusely for a long time. The tears would not stop flowing. I saw Jesus wearing a crown of thorns, bruised, hanging upon the Cross – for me! O such Love, whose depths I would never be able to fully fathom! He took **my** place! I wept tears of thankfulness. All my life it had seemed that nobody ever understood my pain, but Jesus not only understood it, He went through it, and bore it upon Himself, taking it away! He took my sin and my pain away!

The revelation of the Cross changed my life. I saw that the Cross of Jesus is the central theme of the Word of God. Since that day the Cross of Jesus has been the main theme of my life and ministry. The old story of the Cross has never ceased to grip me and fascinate me. Of all the men of God I know, nobody can quite preach it like my friend and brother Reinhard Bonnke. Whenever I listen to him preach the simple Gospel, I begin to cry. I still can't stop crying, today, so many years after I first heard that wonderful story of the Cross of Jesus the first time ever.

Chapter 10

Reaching Out

With the authorities still looking for me, things began to get tough for me in Lahore. I then moved down South to Karachi and lived there as part of a 'colony' of the Children of God. The Children of God always want new members to take new and biblical names to be used instead of their legal names. Some of the choices of names really made one wonder. For example, one man was called 'Habbakuk 2:4' (2:4 being his surname). One young lady called herself 'Ruth the Truth'. Yet another man who was confined to a wheelchair called himself 'Hananiah Ironside', after Hananiah in the Bible and the wheelchair-bound police commissioner Ironside from the popular TV series. I decided upon Isaiah, and that is what I was called from then on. Later on I changed it to Hosanna.

My days were spent reading the Bible, memorising Scripture, telling people about Jesus, handing out tracts. Many Muslims were fascinated by the gospel message of God's love and salvation. They made professions of faith in the Lord Jesus, but wanted to remain 'secret believers' out of fear of persecution and death. I never understood this. We cannot hide our light under a bushel! The Lord Jesus said very plainly,

> *'Whosoever therefore shall confess me before men, him will I confess also before my Father which is in heaven. But whosoever shall deny me before men, him will I also deny before my Father which is in heaven.'*

(Matthew 10:32–33)

I never saw any immoral behaviour of any kind in the group while I lived in the Children of God colony. On the contrary, I saw a real zeal to tell people about Jesus, a real zeal to reach the lost. There were, however, a few other things I noticed. These, to a baby Christian like me, did not appear to be big issues or things that I saw as being neccesarily wrong. Today, however, I can see what great danger lies in them.

Firstly, The COGs had a very extreme, dominant and controlling leader. Moses David controlled and dominated the whole movement. At times it seemed that he was more important than the Lord Jesus Himself. The only thing that mattered was what Moses David said. He decided what everybody should believe. His teachings and 'revelations' set the frame of reference through which we were to interpret Scripture. His teaching, in practice, carried the same weight as the Word of God. There was no room for any questioning of what 'Mo' taught. Today I can see that the whole thing was a cult built around one man, Moses David. He called himself 'King David' and we were like his 'guerilla army'. We took more pride in being his followers than in being followers of Jesus. Somehow, it seemed that our identification with 'Mo' was stronger than our identification with Christ Jesus.

Secondly, the Children of God had a spirit of exclusivism. Some of our teachings and beliefs were 'exclusive', in other words, 'only **we** had the understanding and revelation' of certain spiritual issues. The whole body of Christ was missing it, but we had it! Everybody else was missing God, except us! Others were in the world 'system', we were the ones with the 'new wine in new bottles'! Many in the Children of God were dissatisfied children of ministers from different religious backgrounds, called 'Babylon' or 'The system'. I noticed that we (the COG), were almost the only ones out witnessing on the streets. This made us feel like 'God's Elite Soldiers', far ahead of and better than all others in the 'system'. We were the ones who would bring a 'Revolution for Jesus'! It all seemed and looked that way, but today, older and more mature, I see it as pride and arrogance, deadly sins.

Thirdly, because the Children of God saw themselves as more advanced and superior to other Christians, they found it hard to have anything to do with other believers. Separation was not only from the world, but from other Christians too. We would join others at times, but only if **we** could control, or if we got any advantage out of it. We acknowledged that these other Christians were saved, but that was about all. They couldn't pray as as we could pray! We had a lot to teach them, but they had nothing to teach us! Because of this it was natural that we kept to ourselves, within our own group. Even reading newspapers or magazines, though not totally forbidden, was nevertheless frowned upon.

People living like this for long enough can lose

touch with the rest of the body of Christ, and with reality. Such people get brainwashed and believe they are special and extra-spiritual when in reality, they are way off course! They have no frame of reference outside themselves or their own group. At that time I did not see these things as a danger, because I wanted to submit, humble myself and learn, but today I see these things as some of the probable factors that caused the Children of God to become a cult.

Being oblivious to these things, I relished being part of a team, interacting, learning, doing things together with others. Along with two other brothers, I did a couple of weeks of 'beach ministry' among the hippies at the Hawkes Bay beach on the Arabian Sea coast. There were hordes of them, smoking the cheap and readily available 'hashish', stoned-out every day.

The three of us went out there from Karachi, traveling on the roof of an overloaded bus, together with goats, sheep and chickens. We slept our first night in sleeping bags, under the stars, on the beach. I remember waking up in the morning with a huge black dog lying asleep across my legs. We rented a beach hut with no running water. I was the cook, and made a three-course meal for about 30 people every evening, all this on a single kerosene burner! There was no electricity either, so we used kerosene lanterns. We were excited! The three of us would be out inviting the hippies, then we would sing for them, share the Gospel, feed them my three-course meal, and finally spend the rest of the evening talking to them about Jesus.

On other evangelism projects we would sometimes go out in faith, without food or money, preaching and witnessing to people, sleeping in pup-tents in parks. This was to help us to learn to live by faith in God. I found this very beneficial, as I was soon to find myself in many situations when only a miracle from God could meet my needs. I am happy to be able to say that God always met every need in every situation I found myself in. Never have I ever lacked anything, because God has always been faithful to provide.

We visited schools and witnessed on the streets. At times we ran into Muslim fanatics who would start screaming and ranting at us. A crowd would gather, the fanatics would get them all worked-up, and things would begin to get really dangerous. Just as things would reach boiling point, we would just disappear, regroup in another place, and continue.

Once I was arrested by an plainclothed official from Naval Intelligence. He said that they had been watching us for sometime, and they knew beyond doubt that we were spying for and were financed by the Israeli government! He took me for interrogation to the police 'torture house' in the centre of the city, but God helped me get out of that situation. I just had no fear, so I acted really boldly, and they let me go after apologising profusely!

What I didn't know was all this time my father had the police after me, trying to trace my whereabouts.

Chapter 11

Prisoner for Christ

The police came one afternoon in May 1976 and took my friends and me off for 'questioning'. We were kept for 48 hours without food at the police station while they 'prepared a case' against us. Some very high people from the government were involved, because my father had instigated the whole thing.

The case was finally prepared. We were to be held in 'detention for 90 days, further extendable by an additional 90 days', under the 'Maintenance of Public Order Act' because we were 'distributing anti-Islamic literature, indulging in anti-Islamic activities, and disturbing public peace and order'. We were all sent off to the Karachi Central Jail, where we were kept in the 'Political Prisoners Ward'.

We were issued with filthy blankets stained with the vomit of previous prisoners. On these we had to lie on the rough, uneven brick-paved floor, all five of us in one filthy little cell. Breakfast was a mug of tea with a 'chapatti', a flat round flour tortilla that is staple diet for all Pakistanis. These 'chapattis', however, were baked of flour that was full of sand and tiny pebbles. Lunch and dinner consisted of lentils or vegetables accompanied with the same kind of bread. The toilet was two small concrete blocks with a shoebox-size metal container in between, in the corner of the cell. It was oppressively hot, mosquitoes and other insects feasted on our blood, but we rejoiced, counting it a privilege to be imprisoned for the gospel. I was just a few months old in the Lord, and I felt it such a thrilling previlige to experience what the apostles went through in the book of Acts! It was exciting!

(I thought all Christians went to prison for the Gospel, that it was a part of the normal Christian life. Later on after my release, whenever I was introduced to Christian brethren, I introduced myself as 'Isaiah, just released from prison', and would then proceed to ask them when they had been in prison. This and other things I often said in sheer ignorance brought many chuckles!)

After a couple of days they released the four brothers with me and deported them. I was left alone in prison.

I found a legal clause through which I could get out on bail. The state responded by slapping some really fantastic charges on me. It is not illegal to preach the Gospel, at least on paper, as Pakistan claims to be a country where people of all religions are free to practice and preach their faith. Because of this they had to make up something else to lock me up securely.

This time I was 'detained until further orders', which means, in effect, 'lock him in and throw the key away', under the Defence of Pakistan Rules. I was supposed to be an 'illegal alien', a non-Pakistani who had entered the country for subversive activities! It was impossible for me to prove that I, contrary to the charges, was indeed a Pakistani, because my father had my passport and ID documents safely in his custody. I met some prisoners who had been held innocently imprisoned for **years** under this particular clause!

I wrote to the General Headquarters Army, to the Air Force, to General Zia-ul-Haq, later President, then Chief of Staff (Army), telling them that I was being held illegally and that they should send documents proving that I was, in fact, Pakistani. Nobody replied. As a last resort I wrote my father threatening with a 'Habeas Corpus' in the High Court if he did not get me out immediately. By this time I had been in prison for over two months. Several times I was chained together with other prisoners, and taken to the courts where we waited for hours but nothing ever happened.

My father, upon receiving my threat, came immediately with a release order. The day after my release, a senior police officer informed me of the limitations and restrictions imposed upon me. As an ex-political prisoner, I did not have the right to hold a passport or to leave the country. Secondly, I was put under my father's authority and had to live with him in Lahore, where he now lived. Thirdly, I could not leave Lahore without permission. If I broke these rules, they would send me to prison again. People living in civilized nations may not understand this, but this is exactly how the legal system works in Pakistan. The law is overruled and manipulated by the whims of the powerful, while those without influence have no choice. In spite of these circumstances, I knew that God would get me through. It is good to be hooked up to the King of kings!

Chapter 12

Going Underground

I went to Lahore with my father. I was not allowed to get a job. My father, by now retired, had received a farm for his meritorious service in the army and because he had been decorated for bravery. I was often sent to watch over the farm. He would pay me bus fare, and nothing more, so I never had any extra money.

My father's farm was in a very wild area of the Punjab. The people in the area were known as 'Janglis', meaning 'the wild people'. They were all illegal occupants of government land. Because of this there were no irrigation canals or electricity in the area. These people were renegades, armed and dangerous. Even the police feared them. Murders were common, and there was no law and order in the area. They had their own code of ethics, in which crime was looked at as something positive. Young men, for example, had to prove their manhood by stealing somebody's cattle, or by committing some other crime. Only then would they be considered eligible for marriage!

I lived in a hut on the farm, and was always armed with a loaded rifle or shotgun. I never went to sleep without a weapon by my side. The locals would test me often to see how far they could go. They would steal our wheat and make mischief to intimidate me. It was a real dilemma for me. I had to be strong and respond firmly, yet I did not want to shoot anyone, not even in self-defence. What could I do?

One day they found out that I had just recently been released from prison. In their minds, going to prison was the ultimate sign and achievement of manhood. One of them said to me, 'You were in prison! Only the bravest among the brave end up in prison!'

After this they left me alone!

Months passed. I was forced to go to the mosque, where I was made to go through the motions of Muslim prayer. What they didn't know was that I was praying to Jesus! One of my father's friends offered me his attractive young daughter in marriage if I would become a Muslim again. I was offered a lot of money. I would even get a beautiful wife and my own business. But all I wanted was to get away and follow my precious Jesus.

One thing they could never understand: 'What fault do you find with Islam? Why do you have to leave our religion and follow a "foreign" religion? Tell us, what is wrong with Islam?'

My answer always was, 'I have nothing against you or your religion. I do not even think on these lines, but you must understand, Jesus has gripped me. He has taken a hold of my life. He is calling me. He is so real. He has given me peace, joy, love, he has set me free from my sin and misery. He is real! I would gladly do anything to please you, but I cannot deny Someone who is so wonderfully real and close to me. I would be a fool if I denied Him. Please understand this!'

One of my father's closest friends, a General, once retorted with, 'Ah! All young men get drunk, smoke pot, sow their wild oats, live on the wild side! It's perfectly normal, but then they get a job, marry, mature and stabilize. You don't need this Jesus! Come on, Be real!'

But I had made my choice. For me it was Jesus only, and nothing else.

To understand what I am saying, one has to experience a real blood-washed salvation, really knowing Jesus as a living dynamic reality, so that we know that our sins are forgiven, and our name is written in the Lamb's Book of Life. We must let Jesus grip us, and when He does, He will give us the faith, the will, the power we need. We can then walk through fire without being burnt. Jesus is mighty to give us the victory.

I could not carry my Bible openly as I would then be taken to the police immediately. I found a solution to this problem. I took a 90-minute audio cassette, taped Scripture on one side and music on the other. I would listen to Scripture, and if someone came, turn the tape over and turn on the music!

As an 'underground' Christian, I had managed to make contact with some other believers. George and Anne Tewksbury, Presbyterian missionaries in Lahore, now retired in the USA, showed me much love and kindness. So wonderful is God's love flowing through His people reaching out to one another, loving, comforting and encouraging! I remember visiting them often, as often as I could get away. I was under such pressure and persecution, and badly needed fellowship. George and Anne, though extremely busy missionaries, always had time for me. I watched them minister to young Europeans bound by drugs. They had these addicts, some of them totally insane, staying in their home. It was pathetic to see these young people in the clutches of the devil, being destroyed by drugs. Most of these young men and women came from affluent homes where they had received everything, except love.

One young man who was brought to George and Anne was Francois, the son of a French diplomat in Greece. Francois was insane, his mind destroyed by heavy narcotics. He had been running through the streets stark naked. People had caught him and had beaten him. Somehow a Christian had brought him to George and Anne. The devil may have come to destroy, but Jesus, the mighty Deliverer, came to destroy the works of the devil! In the Book of Amos the Word of God says that if a lion devours a lamb, even to the point where only one ear and one leg are hanging out of the lion's mouth, the Lord can, and shall, still deliver and set free!

I saw Jesus deliver people from the very jaws of death. I remember one particular girl, Karin from Austria. Twenty seven years old, she had been on heroin for 10 years. Her husband had just died of an overdose. She looked like an old woman. Several of her teeth had rotted and fallen out. George and Anne ministered to her with such tenderness, praying with her, that she was totally delivered. I remember her face, radiant with the Light of the Son of God, as beautiful as an angel, with tears streaming down her cheeks, as she used to sing the song,

'And Jesus said, come to the Waters, stand by
    my side;
I know you are thirsty, you won't be denied;
I felt every tear-drop when in darkness you
    cried;

And I strove to remind you, that for those
    tears I died.'

Surely Jesus is a mighty Deliverer! Karin's testimony encouraged me very much, and strengthened my faith in the Lord Jesus.

George and Anne taught me a lot, and prayed with me often. They were people with great spiritual power, yet infinitely meek, tender and compassionate. At times I would tell George what I was going through. He would hold my hand and weep, tears streaming down his cheeks. The love and the strength of God that they imparted into my life kept me going in those difficult days of my life.

My father finally found my New Testament hidden away under my mattress. To make things worse, that particular day was the festival of 'Id', the holiest day of the Muslim year! He was furious.

The police came that evening and took me to the police station. They set out a few chairs in the front yard. My father and the police officers sat while I was made to stand like a common criminal on trial. A crowd soon gathered to see what was happening. My father and the police officers loudly berated me for having become a Christian. They called me names and insulted me loudly. The people who had gathered also joined in the shouting, expressing shock that the son of such a great man as my father could do something so terrible, bringing such disgrace upon his name.

Finally my father took me aside. He used such a filthy invective referring to the Lord Jesus that for the first time in my life, I stood up to him and spoke to him in anger, 'Don't you talk that way about Jesus! You don't realize who He is!' I said.

This, for him, was the last straw. He had done all he could, and had failed. There was now only one thing he could do... 'You should be **beheaded**!', he snapped.

I could not believe what I had just heard. I looked into his eyes, and it suddenly struck me that he actually meant what he had just said. I looked him straight in the eyes and said, 'Alright, go ahead and kill me. I know Jesus is taking me to Heaven. You may kill my body, but you can never, never kill my soul!'

That night I decided there was no way out for me but to leave Pakistan. Political unrest had started in Pakistan. Massive demonstrations had been held on the streets, and the police had shot and killed people by the hundreds. As was the practice, everybody who had ever been arrested under the Defence of Pakistan Rules was being rearrested. This meant that I, who had been a 'political prisoner', could be arrested and jailed at any time, for no reason, and for an indefinite period. In a few weeks, General Zia-ul-Haq, my father's friend, would overthrow the government in a coup. Prime Minister Zulfiqar Ali Bhutto would be arrested and later hanged. The crowds were demanding strict adherence to Islamic law. Religious leaders spoke out openly and demanded total adherence to Islamic law. One cleric even said on television that any Muslim converting to Christianity should be executed. So, on one hand I was threatened by imprisonment once again, and on the other, my own father had just threatened to have me executed!

I had been thinking about leaving the country for some time, but I was not sure if it was God's way for me. Furthermore, I was penniless and knew nobody who could get me out. But now, I was convinced that it was God's will for me to leave Pakistan as soon as possible.

I shared with George and Anne Tewksbury that the time had come for me to leave. They prayed with me, and together we committed my journey into the hands of God.

The time had come for me to leave Pakistan. I knew that the Lord had His hand on me, and that He would make a way. In the Bible He had never let His children down. Surely He would make a way for me.

Chapter 13

Flight to Safety

Early one morning, just as dawn was breaking over Lahore, I made my escape with the help of some Muslim friends who sympathised with me. This was the spring of 1977. I had been a follower of Jesus for 16 months only, but these 16 months had been full of severe persecution. I had been in a mental institution, been arrested a few times, imprisoned and threatened with execution. Now, finally, I was on my way. Carrying my backpack, I made my way to Karachi, where I stayed with some Christian friends. An intensive search was going on for me, but I was well hidden by this family. I found out years later that my father had gone to the Inspector General of Police, the highest ranking police official in the Punjab province, and had told him what to do to me, 'When you catch him you have my permission to kill him – hang him!'

The Christian family I was hiding with managed to get me a passport and gave me 500 US dollars, a small fortune in Pakistan, to help me get away. I stayed with them for over a month, and they treated me like a son. During this time one long-time desire was fulfilled – I was baptised in water. The baptism was done in the sea by American missionary James

Turner. Pastor Turner was found murdered, some months afterwards. Nobody ever caught the killer(s), and nobody could ever ascertain exactly why he was killed.

I found out that it was impossible for a Pakistani to go anywhere without a visa, with the exception of Turkey. Also, it was practically impossible to get a visa for anywhere, but Afghanistan! So I made up my mind that I would go to Afghanistan, then to Turkey, and finally 'west'. I had the notion that since 'all white people were Christians', I would certainly be welcome in 'Christian nations' like England or the USA! All I wanted was to live in a place where I could read my Bible and worship and serve God in a peaceable way without being arrested for it!

The Embassy of Afghanistan stamped a 10-day visa on my passport. After this I spent 120 dollars on an air ticket to Kabul-Istanbul (via Moscow), on Aeroflot, the Soviet Airlines. They were the cheapest I could find. I found out that it was illegal for a Pakistani to take US dollars or any other foreign currency to Afghanistan so I hid the money in my socks.

I caught a train to Quetta, a city over 600 miles away, and about 70 miles from the Afghan border.

The manhunt for me was still on.

Chapter 14

The Way Out

In Quetta I ran into an army major with whom I had shared a bunker while I was with the infantry battalion in Kashmir. This officer invited me to stay in his home. So there I was, safely in an army officer's house in a military cantonment, while a manhunt was going on for me! The officer put me in touch with another major who was commanding some troops in Chaman, a small town where the Pakistan-Afghan border crossing was.

I arrived in Chaman by bus, and went straight to the army officers' mess. I met the major, who happened to be in civilian clothes when I came. I was eager to get out of Pakistan as soon as possible, so he took me straight to the Pakistan Police and Immigration checkpost. The police officer on duty examined my travel documents, shook his head, and refused to let me through because I did not have a letter from my home police station stating that I was not wanted by the police! While this was going on, another police officer began to look through a thick file where they had pictures and descriptions of 'wanted' people. My picture was in there!

The major suddenly intervened and said, 'This man is with me, and he is going through! I'll sign a paper on his behalf now. Send it to my office tomorrow and I'll put my official stamp on it!' They let me through without any delay. I just praised the Lord!

The next obstacle was the Pakistan Customs. As a matter of routine, they normally asked everybody to declare any foreign currency one might be carrying. I had my US dollars hidden away in my socks. If I told the truth, I'd be arrested, but if I lied, I felt like God would withdraw His blessing and protection from me! I was in a real dilemma, and in silent prayer committed the matter to my heavenly Father.

When I finally stood before the Customs Officer, he looked at me and asked, 'Are you Mr Alam?' I said I was. He made a little 'X' on my backpack saying, 'I have just received a telephone call, and have been instructed to let you through without any questions.'

I was stupefied, the major looked stunned. We stared at each other. Who could have called? Nobody else but the two of us knew we were there!

Then I understood. It must be my Heavenly Father! Somewhere by the Throne He has a telephone for special situations like the one I was in!

The customs post was out in the middle of the desert, and between there and the Afghan Immigration point-of-entry was a few miles of no-mans-land. There was no public transportation, and I was wondering how I'd ever get to Afghanistan. As these thoughts coursed through my mind, the major and I noticed two gentlemen who drove in, in a flashy new Mercedes-Benz with diplomatic plates. They stepped into the customs post. They proved to be the Consul-General of Iran and his assisstant. With no other visible alternative, I asked them for a ride!

They stared at me unbelievingly, and eyed me

from my head down to my toes. I stood there, looking like a hippie, long-haired, unshaven, wearing grubby jeans, carrying a backpack and guitar. I certainly did not look like the kind of fellow that diplomats would give a ride to in their nice Mercedes! They conferred amongst themselves, all the time keeping an eye on me. As they spoke, in their native Persian, I picked up a few words like 'hashish', 'hippie' etc, but suddenly they said, 'OK, hop in, we'll take you to Kandahar!' Kandahar was the first big city in Afghanistan, from there I'd take a bus to Kabul to catch the flight to Istanbul, changing planes in Moscow.

I got in the car, and we drove off. We soon arrived at the Afghan Immigration check-point. The officers glanced at the Iranians' diplomatic passports and saluted. Then they looked at my Pakistani passport, at me, at the Mercedes. I knew what they were thinking! The officer looking at my Afghan visa shook his head and said that my visa, unfortunately, was not in order. Under no circumstances could they let me into Afghanistan. To my surprise, the Iranian diplomats spoke up, 'This man is our friend! You must let him in, and we'll take the responsibility to see that everything is sorted out right!' The officers saluted and let us drive into Afghanistan.

'Thank you Jesus,' I whispered, as we drove into Afghanistan, at the foot of the majestic Spin Baldak mountains. I took the breath of freedom. God was with me, I was out of Pakistan! He was taking me through!

Chapter 15

Further Complications

We arrived in Kandahar where the Iranian diplomats dined me royally in two different and very nice restaurants! Then they put me on a bus to Kabul.

I arrived in Kabul and checked into a cheap little hotel on the famous 'Chicken Street'. The next thing I did was to try to locate the local Children of God colony. I finally found them but felt that there was something strange about them. It was hard to put what I felt into words, but something just did not seem to be right. Perhaps, I thought, it was because I had not had any contact with them for so long. I asked one of the brothers for the 'Mo letters' I had missed. 'Mo letters' were booklets and leaflets containing teachings from the Children of God's leader, Moses David. The Mo letters I had seen in my couple of months living with the Children of God were mostly very basic. Now, in Kabul, I was given a stack of fresh Mo letters to look through, and was horrified to see that most of the letters were nothing but filthy pornography, some encouraging fornication and adultery, while some were downright blasphemous.

I felt so hurt, lonely and confused. It was through these people I had come to know Jesus. How could this happen? What could cause these wonderful brothers and sisters to sink so low into the pit from which they once had been delivered?

Reeling from this shock, and needing fellowship, I began to look for 'normal' Christians. God led me to some foreign believers who worked in Kabul. I told them I was going to Turkey, and they gave me the names of an American couple who were working as underground missionaries with Operation Mobilisation. I went to Aeroflot, the Soviet Airline with which I held a ticket. They informed me that since I had a 4–5 day layover in Moscow I needed a Soviet Visa. I was refered to the Soviet Embassy who told me that as my passport was not valid for the USSR, I could not be granted a visa!

I came back to the hotel, and prayed, asking the Lord to help me. I did not want to tangle with the Russians, as I had just finished reading a book called *Vanja* by Myrna Grant, telling about how brutally the Communists persecuted Christians. It was horrifying.

I went back to the Aeroflot office. I knew in the back of my mind that Aeroflot offices overseas are normally manned by KGB agents. This was common knowledge. At the Aeroflot office I spoke to the lady who received me and informed her that I had been refused a Soviet Visa.

She said that in that case I would not be allowed to board the flight, and also that my ticket was non-refundable.

'Lady,' I said, 'I want you to know that I am a Christian, and have escaped from Pakistan where I was persecuted for my faith in Jesus Christ. If you don't let me go to Russia, I'll be sent back to Pakistan where I face prison and death!'

She said, 'Wait a moment!' and went to the desk of a smartly-dressed man who seemed to be the person in charge of the place. I could hear them talking, and pointing at me.

The smartly-dressed man stepped out from behind his desk and came to me. He and the lady smiled at me understandingly. He said, 'Everything is going to be OK. Don't worry.' He then picked up the phone, called the Soviet Embassy and spoke to someone for a short while. 'Just go to the embassy, someone is waiting for you, and you'll get the visa,' he said to me.

I praised the Lord all the way to the embassy!

A gray-suited gentleman received me at the embassy as if I was a visiting dignitary. I did not fully comprehend what was going on, but I had a 5-day visa issued in 10 minutes. It normally would take two weeks to get it.

With God nothing is impossible!

Chapter 16

Refreshed in Moscow

I boarded the Aeroflot aircraft at Kabul Airport, arriving in Moscow some hours later. Aeroflot took me to their hotel in the city where they gave me a room and a 'meal coupon' for a complimentary lunch.

Walking into the restaurant, I noticed that every single table was taken, but right by the door, where I stood, was a table with three people and three empty chairs. I asked the dark-haired gentleman who seemed to be looking at me intently if I could join them. 'Sure, just make yourself at home!', he said.

As soon as I sat down, he began to talk and talk. He asked me all kinds of questions, who I was, where I was coming from, ... etc.

I was not too eager to answer all his questions. He definitely looked a KGB type to me, and I certainly was not planning on a one-way trip to Siberia! Yet I answered all his questions honestly, fearing that God would stop blessing me if I lied. I finally told him that I was a refugee, fleeing persecution because of my faith in Jesus. 'Brother, praise the Lord!' he exclaimed, grabbing my hand and shaking it vigourously. 'I am also a Christian!'

'Where are you from?', I asked him.

'Sweden,' he replied. I looked at him and thought

that he certainly did not look very Swedish to me with his dark hair!

I suddenly remembered what a Baptist missionary in Pakistan had told me just before I had left the country, 'If you ever run into any Swedish Christians from the "Orebro Mission", ask them to help you. They are good people.' I had made a note of this in my little address book. So I turned to this dark-haired Swede and asked him, 'Do you know of the Orebro Mission?'

As I said this his jaw dropped open and his spaghetti fell out of his mouth. He pulled out his wallet and showed me his calling card. It said 'Thord-Ove Thordsson, **Orebro Mission**'! This man was one of the leaders of the Orebro Mission! God has a wonderful way of leading His people. He brought me all the way to Moscow, the world headquarters of communism, to meet a minister of Jesus Christ!

Thord-Ove said, 'You don't know this, but I saw you at the airport in Kabul. We were on the same flight to Moscow. I sensed that there was something special about you, and I felt that I had to speak to you, but I couldn't. There were so many other people around. When you walked into the restaurant and asked to sit next to us, I figured that God was in all this, and I just had to find out who you were. Now I know. I want us to keep in touch, and I'll help you as much as I can.'

Thord-Ove and I had wonderful fellowship in Moscow. We worshipped, prayed and took the Lord's Supper together in my hotel room. He gave me some US dollars as a gift, and paid for my hotel room, as Aeroflot gave me only one night's free accomodation. Then we parted our ways. He flew on to Stockholm, Sweden, and I to Istanbul, Turkey.

Chapter 17

Istanbul, Turkey

Arriving in Istanbul I found a place to stay in a cheap, seedy area recommended to me by a fellow backpacker. It was infested with shady people who were dealing in narcotics and black-marketing in travellers cheques. One fellow-Pakistani offered me a British Passport with a German Residence Permit stamped on it, an air ticket to Germany plus 400 pounds sterling, if I would deliver a package for him to a friend. In other words, smuggling drugs.

I did not know how to find the Operation Mobilisation missionaries, and I wanted to get away from the area where I was staying as fast as possible. With this in mind, I started looking for a church, walking for hours, and I finally found a Roman Catholic church. The priest, a very kind man, fed me a hearty meal and spent two whole days with me, feeding me at his own expense, encouraging me and helping me to find the American couple who were with Operation Mobilisation. I stayed with this couple at their home for three weeks. They were very kind, loving and hospitable towards me.

While in Istanbul I met the Children of God again. I felt terrible just being around them. I battled with my conflicting emotions towards them. On the one hand, if it wasn't for them, I would probably never have heard about my Lord Jesus. On the other hand, they had lost their first love and now seemed full of unclean spirits, which to me was totally unacceptable. Yet, it seemed to me that my bonds with them were so strong that I just could not totally break away from them. I felt that I owed them so much.

I then found out that they had a new doctrine that encouraged prostitution 'to win converts!' I also saw a 'Mo letter' in which Moses David proudly took credit for the recent great air disaster in Tenerife. Two 747 aircraft had collided on the runway at the airport and hundreds had lost their lives. Moses David had been deported from there some time earlier, and now he claimed, this was 'divine retribution' for deporting a 'prophet of God'. I was sickened by all this and shared this with the couple I was staying with. They advised me to break with the Children of God completely and decisively, and with all my heart.

I struggled with it, but because I loved Jesus so much and wanted to distance myself from sin, I made a definite decision to renounce and break all ties with them. It was painful, but I wrote a letter to my old Children of God leaders in Dubai. I urged them to repent of their sin, and turn to the Lord. Furthermore, I informed them that I no longer wished to be associated with them. It hurt to break ties with those who had led me to the Lord, but I loved Jesus more than anything else, so I chose to put Him first. After I had done it, I felt uncontaminated, pure and free again.

Chapter 18

Divine Intervention

The American couple I was staying with had, in the meantime, arranged for Operation Mobilisation to invite me to their annual summer campaign and con- ference in Leuven, Belgium. I thus received a Belgian visa, and with the money I had plus a gift from my American hosts, I bought a ticket to Brussels. The Lord was making the way for me, but suddenly I realized that I had one big problem. It was 1977, and European countries required that visitors arriving from third-world countries could show at least 200 dollars upon arrival, to ensure that they were bonafide visitors, and not penniless illegal immigrants. The trouble was that I had only about 5 or 7 dollars left after my ticket was paid for.

The Lord had earlier impressed upon me, after I left Pakistan, not to ask anybody for any money, so I was very careful not to advertise my financial needs, but to trust Him alone. I prayed and committed the situation to Him who watches over us with such love, and meets every need.

I went to Istanbul's Yesilkoy airport and stood in the check-in area. The financial need hovered in the background. I needed 200 dollars, and fast!

'Hi brother!' It was an American brother I had

met a couple of times in Istanbul. He knew nothing of my financial need. 'I heard you were leaving today, so I felt I had to come to see you off!'

We chatted until my flight was announced. We shook hands, and I felt some paper rustle in his grip as we shook hands. 'I just felt that I had to give you this!' he said as he pressed the 'paper' into my hand. I looked. It was 200 dollars in two 100 dollar bills! I began to praise God, and danced all the way to the waiting aircraft!!

Surely Jesus is alive today and takes care of His people!

Chapter 19

Operation Mobilisation

Upon arrival at Zaventem airport in Brussels, I went straight to Operation Mobilisation's headquarters not very far from there.

I was very warmly received by the brethren. The very first thing that I felt was that God inspired me to give away all my money, to the last cent. I did so, and stood there without a cent in my pocket.

I spent two months with an Operation Mobilisation summer team in Ostend, witnessing, testifying, singing every day on the streets, and on the beautiful beaches all along the picturesque Belgian coast. Every home in the province of West Flanders received a Gospel of Mark.

We lived in an old house close to the beach, sleeping in sleeping bags on the floor, 10 of us in a room. We were a total of 28 people in the team. We learnt a lot, fellowshipped, and were happy and excited, doing what we all loved to do more than anything else in the world – telling people about Jesus!

There were drug-dealers and others who did not like my testimony and what I shared in the street meetings. Some of them called me names, threatened me and tried to intimidate me. One of the things we preached about was that Jesus could deliver drug addicts.

I remember one particular young man called Jean. He had used heavy drugs for many years and rode with a motorcycle gang. He looked ferocious, with long hair down to his waist, wearing wraparound mirror sunglasses and a black leather jacket covered with steel studs. He would stand there every day at our street meetings, glowering. I made contact with him and shared with him every day. He was hard and cold as steel. One day he took his sunglasses off. I was struck dumb as I looked into his eyes. Never before in my life had I ever seen such eyes, so hard and so icy-cold. The days went by, and I kept at it, witnessing and sharing with him about Jesus.

Suddenly one day, as I was talking to Jean, God let me see him as he really was: bound by fear and tormented. I said to him, 'Jean, you want to receive Jesus, but there is one thing holding you back, and that is fear. You are afraid that if you give your life to Jesus, your motorcycle-gang friends will beat you up with knuckledusters and chains. Isn't that true?'

He looked down at the ground and nodded silently. At that moment the love and compassion of Jesus filled my heart, and I said to him, 'Jean, Jesus suffered so much in order to save you, no suffering that we could ever endure could match the intensity of His pain and suffering; but I want to show you how much Jesus loves you ... If you receive the Lord Jesus, I will stand before your friends and take your beating. Would that convince you that Jesus loved you enough to die for you?'

His eyes welled up with tears, and right there, on the beach promenade, Jean knelt and asked the Lord Jesus to come into his heart.

The next day he came over to our house and one of the team gave him a haircut! He accompanied us to church. He was a new man! The Bible says that,

> *'Therefore if any man be in Christ, he is a new creature: old things are passed away; behold, all things are become new!'*   (2 Corinthians 5:17)

After Belgium I spent one month with friends in the old-fashioned fishing village of Urk in Holland. My time in Operation Mobilisation was very fruitful. I got to know George Werver, the founder and leader of the movement. George was and remains today, a man of faith and great vision, imparting to thousands of youth a vision for the lost. He had a powerful emphasis on surrendering one's life totally to God for the sake of the gospel. George lived a simple lifestyle, and his one passion was the spreading of the Gospel all over the world. He left a powerful impression on my life, a fire that still burns in my heart today. I dedicated my life afresh for the work of the Gospel.

The greatest thing that happened to me at Operation Mobilisation was that God opened my eyes to world missions, and put a fresh desire and passion for souls into my heart.

Chapter 20

Sweden

At the end of three months in Operation Mobilisation, as their summer programme drew to a close, I received a letter from Thord-Ove Thordsson, the Swedish brother I had met in Moscow. He had worked very hard to help me get to Sweden and was pleased to inform me that the Orebro Mission, together with the Capernwray Fellowship of Torchbearers, had granted me a scholarship to attend the Torchbearers' Bible School in Holsbybrunn, Sweden. It was an English-language school with mostly overseas students.

I did not have any money to travel to Sweden and did not advertise my need, but all of a sudden I began to get envelopes stuffed with money from anonymous donors. I believe it was God blessing me back for giving away the 200 dollars I had when I first came to Belgium. I soon had quite a sizable sum of money, plus an offer of a free all-expenses-paid ride all the way to Sweden in an air-conditioned Mercedes!

I arrived in Sweden in style, praising the Lord for His goodness, on the 23rd of September 1977.

I immediately fell in love with Sweden. I thought then, and still think it to be one of the loveliest countries on earth. I found Swedish believers to be shy, yet warm, friendly, and generous once one got to know them. One thing that impressed me very much was the average Swedish Christian's strong sense of separation from the world and commitment to God. In many other countries it is socially popular to be a church-goer. Most church-goers in those countries thus do not have that strong a sense of being separated from the world. It is fashionable to say, 'I am a Christian'. In Sweden, though, it is the other way around. Church-going is not very fashionable. It is looked upon as something for those out-of-step with modern times, like a relic from the middle-ages for the weak-minded. So those who call themselves Christians are, on the average, very committed and live lives separated from the world. Though generally not very emotional people, I saw in the Swedes a depth, a richness and a trueness that I have always found very precious and beautiful.

The Bible school was located right in the middle of the scenic and thickly wooded rolling countryside of Smaland, in southern Sweden. I had, from some Swedes, heard that the woods were thick with polar bears. It took me several months before I found out that the Swedes were just pulling my leg! Only then did I ever venture into the woods alone. The year at Capernwray was good, and though my heart was not so much into academics, I learnt a lot.

I had never yet received any teaching on giving, tithing or financial blessings. Still, God prompted me to anonymously bless other students with the money I had with me from Belgium. I would secretly put money into their mail-boxes when nobody was around. Amazing things happened. The more money I gave away, the more I received, as a result of which I never lacked anything, and always had enough for 'extras' for myself and to treat and bless my friends! I learnt that we can never outgive God! He always blesses, and blesses over and abundantly!

Because of the influence Operation Mobilisation had on my life, I was all out for soulwinning. At times I acted very immaturely and foolishly, but my instructors at Bible School were very generous and forgiving. Although I definitely was not one of their best students, they encouraged me and corrected me. I participated in as many evangelistic outreaches as I could, witnessing on the streets of the nearby town of Vetlanda, on trains, in schools, prisons and in Church-run coffee houses. I even managed to get a team to minister aboard a US Navy destroyer docked at the Royal Swedish Naval Base in Karlskrona!

At the end of my year at the Bible School, with my Swedish student's visa about to expire, I had to think of my future. I did not want to continue indefinitely as a refugee on the run. A letter had just reached me from Pakistan, saying that the authorities there knew of my whereabouts, that my Swedish visa was soon to expire, and that they were expecting me to return soon! An army officer had also visited the Christian family that had helped me to escape, and had questioned them about me.

I took this to the Lord in prayer, and then decided to seek political asylum in Sweden. My goal, initially, had been to go to an English-speaking country. I did not speak a word of Swedish, and the Swedish language had, it seemed to me, certain humanly unpronounceable sounds. I definitely had no desire to learn Swedish! But on the other hand, I felt that God had brought me to Sweden. I had grown to love the country and the wonderful Swedish Christians. I had developed some deep friendships here, and some of these friends are still very close to me today. They helped me very much spiritually through their love and friendship. I am so grateful to the Lord for them, and for my teachers at Bible School, and the many other wonderful people who prayed for me, encouraged me, and left a lasting deposit of blessings in my life.

Chapter 21

Political Asylum

I went to the Swedish police and applied for political asylum on the grounds of religious persecution in my home country. I also moved right after Bible School to Uppsala. A lawyer was assigned to my case, Mr Peter Nobel, a famous lawyer from the Nobel family, to present my case for political asylum to the Department of Immigration.

I had several long sessions with Mr Nobel, a very kind, intelligent, eloquent and sympathetic man. He prepared my case. We went through the details of my case several times. In the end, when he had prepared my case, he pointed out several important legal aspects to me. He told me that my chances of getting political asylum in Sweden were practically nil, because, according to the Geneva Convention for refugees, a person seeking asylum had to do so in the first signatory (to the convention) country that he came to after leaving his home country. In my case that first country had been Turkey. Furthermore, I had set foot in Belgium, the Netherlands, Germany, Denmark, Norway and Finland before I applied for asylum in Sweden.

Also, an asylum seeker had to apply for asylum within 48 hours of his arrival in the country. I had been in Sweden for about eight months before contacting the police.

Thirdly, there was no known persecution of Christians in Pakistan. I therefore did not come from a recognized 'refugee problem' situation. This was true in a way, because Pakistanis coming from a 'Christian background', though discriminated against and treated like second class human beings by the Muslim majority, had never really been brutally repressed. At the same time, Muslims who turned to Christ were normally killed by their own relatives, but the total number of these cases was not large enough to attract international attention.

These were the factors Mr Nobel spelt out to me. Two other factors were the media reports of thousands of Pakistanis seeking political asylum in Germany on fraudulent grounds, having been deported to Pakistan by the planeload. Also, a couple of years earlier, a Pakistan Air Force aircraft had come to Sweden in an official capacity and Swedish authorities had found drugs aboard the aircraft. So I knew that Pakistanis definitely didn't enjoy a very high level of credibility in Western Europe.

During this time I visited an organisation of lawyers in Stockholm in order to get some 'extra' advice. A lady lawyer who received me asked me very bluntly 'Do you have a Swedish girlfriend?' I answered in the negative, at which she looked at me as if I was weird or abnormal.

'So long in Sweden and no girlfriend!' she exclaimed, her face betraying her amazement, 'your only chance is this: go to a discotheque, meet a girl, start living together with her, and you'll easily get residence and work permits in Sweden.'

I told her that I was a Christian and could not do such a thing.

'Look, when it comes to matters of life and death you have to put religion aside, be realistic.'

I told her, 'God has brought me so far, He can take care of me. But, if I am deported back to Pakistan, if I am killed, I know where I am going when I die, but I will never sin just to get to stay here!'

She said, 'Look, I'm only trying to help. You do it your way. If it does not help, you can always come back here...'

I left her office, went out on the street, and wept. My tears blurred the sights of beautiful Stockholm. Passers-by stared at me. I lifted my face to heaven, and said loudly, 'Jesus, help me! I am trusting you, I want to be faithful to you unto death!'

The devil will always present us with opportunities to compromise, and to take, what seems, to be 'the easy-way-out', but Jesus, the one the Bible calls faithful and true, is the Way. The Way in to the presence of God, the Way out of sin and trouble!

As he mailed off my case to the Immigration Department, Mr Nobel told me that I should be prepared for a **long** wait before the Department of Immigration decided on my case. This seemed plausible, because I had witnessed to a number of refugees in Uppsala who had been waiting as long as two years, some even more, to get a decision on their cases.

In addition, Mr Nobel advised me to be realistic, and not too optimistic. But reality, to the child of God, is that Jesus, the King of kings is upon the throne. The Father has given Him all power in heaven and on earth! This makes impossibilities possibilities, and puts the miraculous abilities and power of God, within our reach!

I told Mr Nobel that I was trusting Jesus. I settled down to wait for the Immigration Department to make their decision, having no idea how long it would take...

Four days later I received a letter from the Immigration Department informing me that I had been granted residence and work permits in Sweden. It was four days since Mr Nobel had sent off my case and it had taken them only two days to decide my case!

Everybody said it was a miracle. I thanked and praised the Lord for His goodness. My long journey had brought me all the way to this wonderful country. Since the day I met Jesus three years earlier, through all the persecution, it had been battles, excitement and victory, together with Jesus! Through Him we are surely more than conquerors!

Chapter 22

Settling Down

I began to settle down in my new homeland, Sweden. The government put me into a language school to learn Swedish. I dreaded it at first, but immersed in a 'Swedish-only' situation I began to pick it up quite well.

Those days, going to the Lutheran church, I did a lot of witnessing, and helped a couple of local ministers in their outreach to refugees and immigrants from the Muslim world. Today I realize that I was probably more of a nuisance than a help! These two brothers, Lars Berntsson and Börje Egfors were very meek and loving people. I spent a lot of time with them and their families. They attended the Lutheran church, so that was where I went too.

In the Lutheran church I met a pretty girl studying at a school of nursing. Her name was Britta. She had been a believer since early childhood, growing up in a small community in the North of Sweden. She had lived faithful to Jesus all her life. With a very tender spirit, she carried around her an air of sweetness and purity. We were just friends at first, but on a trip to England I found myself attracted to her more and more. I fought very hard to suppress my feelings, until finally I was totally sold out. I was crazy about her. I just could not help it, but just being around her would cause my heart to pound and my knees turn to jelly. I was head over heels in love! I felt that she was God's gift to me. I expressed my feelings for her, and we began to spend a lot of time together.

After a 'decent' wait I decided to ask her to marry me. I had prepared a big speech, had planned to propose on my right knee, but my throat would turn dry every time I wanted to pop the big question. Finally, one day, very casually, I found myself blurting out, 'Honey, let's go and get us some rings, eh?'

She accepted, and we were officially engaged on the 18th of May 1979, and were married exactly six months later.

When we started going out together, one of the first things I shared with Britta was, 'I love you very much, and I would rather spend the rest of my life together with you than with anyone else, but you have to know this. I have the call of God on my life. There will come a day when I'll be gone often, preaching the Gospel. I cannot offer you a cosy, "normal" lifestyle, and though I love you very much, Jesus will always come first in my life. If you accept this, we can get married. If not, it's better we call it off, no matter how much it hurts. I love you.'

Britta accepted. Today she is my wife, my help-meet and, apart from Jesus, my very best friend. I love her so much, I would never be what I am without her love and support. The Lord has blessed us with three wonderful children, Immanuel, Victoria and Gabriel. To Jesus I give all the glory for putting her by my side, for giving me a family.

After I finished my language studies in mid-1979, I thought I was ready to get into full-time ministry. I had the calling since I first received Jesus, over three years earlier! God told me to get a job instead. In Uppsala jobs were very hard to come by, but the Lord led me to ask my Swedish language teacher for help. She referred me to one of her friends who promised me a job.

I thought I would get a fancy job, but what I became was a janitor! I found this very humbling. I came from a well-to-do background. We had our own janitor in Pakistan who cleaned our house daily. As a child I could remember having half-a-dozen servants at our beck and call. I had never cleaned floors, and now I was a janitor! Furthermore, Britta was a Registered Nurse, a better and higher-paid job than mine. All my friends had good jobs, and I was a janitor! I felt humiliated and ashamed.

Then the Lord spoke to me. He told me that before he could use me I had to humble myself and learn to get my hands dirty. I janitored for the next 13 months until the Lord brought me to place where I was actually proud to be a janitor! I cleaned those toilets and floors full of gusto and enthusiasm. This was another great life lesson that the Lord was teaching me. I learnt the dignity of labour, and that God looks not at your social status, but at your heart. He is not a respecter of persons, worldly fame or position. If we are proud of what we are in the world, He has to bring us down and break us before he ever begin to use us for His Glory.

I took pride in my work! The people who worked in the offices where I cleaned complimented me in my work. I felt like Leonardo da Vinci being complimented on painting the Sistine Chapel!

Chapter 23

Then the Fire Fell

There was one thing that had bothered me a lot for some time, and that was the lack of power in the Church. The New Testament was full of the supernatural power of God; signs, wonders and miracles, but I did not see that power in any church that I knew. Where was the power? Many ministers put forth bombastic theological explanations saying that God's supernatural power is not for today. Healings and miracles are relegated to today's medical treatments, and prophecy is relegated to 'good teaching', but to me it all amounted to trying to justify unbelief. A lot was being preached about the reasons why God did not do the same things today as in New Testament times, but nobody, it seemed, was teaching us how to get hold of God's power for today! Even soulwinning, the heartbeat of God, was relegated to being something of minor importance.

It seemed that the church lived only for itself, for its own theology, and to entertain its members, keeping them happy, and maintaining the status quo. In my own life too, there was a great lack of power. I witnessed a lot but saw very few results. Some told me that the answer was the 'Baptism with the Holy Spirit', something that seemed to set people called 'Charismatics' apart from other Christians. I then took a closer look at these 'Charismatics', and noticed the following.

They spoke in tongues, prophesied at times, jerked, shook and made a lot of noise, but where was the real power? They were as powerless as anybody else!

They acted as though they were first class Christians, and the rest of the body of Christ was second class. They were better than everybody else. The Bible calls it 'pride'. The power still wasn't there.

I did not mean to mock or be sacriligious, but I was and still am a realist. I was tired of religious talk and games. Paul said that *'The Gospel came not only in word, but in power.'* I heard the words, but did not see the Power.

Being an ignorant young Christian, I came to the conclusion that there couldn't possibly be a specific experience of the 'Baptism with the Holy Spirit' because except for the noise and the shaking, I had the Holy Ghost as much as anyone Pentecostal or Charismatic! Both salvation and the so-called Baptism with the Holy Spirit were surely one and the same thing!

Where was the power?

I became so obsessed and uptight about these things, that I used to get very angry and argumentative with people who even happened to mention the 'Baptism with the Holy Spirit' in my presence.

Around that time I began to have attacks of depression. This depression was rooted in my own insecurity, which would rear its ugly head at times, and also in the spiritual questions I was seeking answers to and battling with. **I wanted to see God's power!**

One day, as I was alone at home, an Ethiopian

minister, Tolesa Gudina, came to visit me. He was a man who lived closer to the face of God than most men I know. Jesus oozed out of every pore of his being. He never strove or argued with anyone, the very opposite of me; His very presence made me feel like a sinner! As he entered our little apartment, Tolesa saw my depressed look, and in a low yet commanding voice, very unlike his normal self, said to me, **'Get down on your knees!'** I obeyed quickly.

Then he put his hands on my head and said in a soft, gentle voice, 'Father, fill him with the Holy Spirit.'

Before I could open my mouth to argue, something like a warm bolt of lightning hit the top of my head, passed through me in a flash, and out through my feet. I found myself worshipping Jesus in other tongues. Wave after wave of the glory of God came over me. I was caught up, worshipping Him who loved me and died for me! I felt Jesus in the room! I felt the surge of Pentecostal power.

My very being was on **fire**! Holy Ghost and fire!

I was baptised with Pentecostal Fire! I experienced it as the disciples did on the day of Pentecost!

God took me out of the realm of human theological argumentation, and into the realm of divine experience, confirming His Word in my life. Now I knew Jesus not only as my Saviour, but also as the one who had baptised me with the Holy Ghost and with fire.

After this a number of our friends received the Holy Spirit in our little apartment, including our pastor's wife. I remember an occasion when as we prayed with a friend to receive the Holy Spirit, the power of God came down so strongly even the living room furniture shook!

Chapter 24

Set Free!

Two other things happened at about the same time that changed my life. The first had to do with my total deliverance from my bouts of depression. Although the baptism with the Holy Spirit had brought me into a new dimension of power and understanding of the Word of God, I still suffered from depression, though far less often. I was partially free.

One day, as I sat there, feeling sorry for myself, God spoke to me and said, 'Go to Elisabeth Larsson (the fiancée of a friend of mine), and get her saved!'

I replied,'Me Lord? Getting someone saved? I feel like I could with some salvation myself!' But God spoke once more, so I got up, changed, and went.

Two hours later the girl was saved! Oh, the joy that filled me at seeing this sinner saved! It was indescribable! People had talked to me, counselled me, cast devils out of me, nothing had helped but this! All I did was lead someone to Jesus, and I had instant victory!

That was the last depression I ever had, in early 1980.

When nothing else works, try to find someone

lost, that is, someone worse off than you are, and tell them about Jesus! Victory is guaranteed!

I was so tired of the devil running me around. That day I decided that I'd chase the devil, instead of him chasing me.

The second thing that happened was that a brother running a Christian bookstore gave me a a couple of books by someone called Kenneth E. Hagin. These books were different to anything I had ever read before. I liked Kenneth Hagin's message of faith, about believing God's Word to change circumstances, to get out of defeat and into victory.

Kenneth Hagin's message on the Integrity of God's Word, and on having faith in God, had a profound impact on my way of thinking. My spiritual life was totally changed, and I found myself moving and walking in a totally new dimension in the things of God. I soon got hold of a lot of such faith-building material, and spent a lot of time reading, studying the Word of God, in prayer and in worship. I sensed the surge of increasing faith in my inner being. I spent a lot of time reading these books, listening to the tapes and praying.

Kenneth Hagin's books made me very hungry for the Word of God. I saw in in the Bible things that I had never seen before. God's promises were for today, and we did not have to make any excuses for not seeing his power. We could see the same miracles and blessings today that we read of in the Word of God!

These books taught me the ABC's of God's promises in the Bible, and of getting hold of God's promises by faith. The power of God was so real now that I began to see healings take place as I prayed for friends who happened to get sick. Kenneth Hagin's books taught me about faith, the key to God's miracle power. In addition, God had used his teaching to totally revolutionise and transform my Christian life, bringing me into a new dimension of faith and power with God.

Chapter 25

Signs and Wonders

It was around this time, in the summer of 1980, that I entered the work of the ministry on a full-time basis. I worked full-time, but was paid no salary, so I trusted the Lord to meet our needs. God showed Himself faithful in every way.

I was fascinated by God's healing power, as I saw it in action. I also learned some hard lessons. The first cancer patient I prayed for died. I had stood up in my home church, full of sceptics and doubters, and announced that the girl dying of cancer would be healed. She died. One can imagine how the sceptics gloated and how I felt. I sought the Lord, and he pointed out the following things:

Firstly, I had more enthusiasm than faith. Faith produces enthusiasm, but mere enthusiasm by itself is not faith. Secondly, I was moved more by 'me getting a miracle', than by compassion for the girl. Thirdly, I had pride. I had announced her impending healing bombastically, in pride, with the emphasis on 'my' ability to pray for the sick, rather than proclaiming the healing power and compassion of Jesus.

I had to repent. The Lord then said, 'Let God be true, and every man a liar!' I chose to believe God's Word inspite of what had happened, because Jesus, and not I, is the healer. This was a stinging and hard-learned lesson.

I began to step up witnessing, people began to get saved in good numbers, and God began to work outstanding healings and miracles. I worked with SESG, the Swedish branch of the Inter-Varsity fellowship. We saw a good number of students and other people giving their lives to Jesus. Uppsala University is a stronghold of worldly humanism and intellectualism, but the Spirit of God pierced through the darkness in many peoples' hearts and minds and they turned to Jesus. Many backsliders rededicated their lives to Jesus. Incurably sick people were healed, the demon-possessed were delivered, the oppressed set free.

Somebody gave me a book teaching about the Name of the Lord Jesus. This book enlightened my heart about that Name that is above every Name. I caught a glimpse of the power, the majesty of that worthy name, **Jesus**. It was as if the Lord had opened my eyes to a whole new dimension of His power. It was for me yet another life-changing revelation from God's Word. I saw that the very mention of the Name of the Lord Jesus would cause sickness, diseases and demons to flee. So great is the power of that Name that the human mind cannot even comprehend or grasp its fullness with its limited understanding!

God just seemed to be blessing more and more with a continuous flow of miracles and healings.

On one occasion I ministered in a little church in southern Sweden where I prayed for a totally lame boy in the powerful Name of Jesus. The doctors had said that he was the third known case in the whole world with that particular kind of infirmity. There was no medicine that could cure him. But with God nothing is impossible. The Bible declares that 'the things that are impossible with man are possible with God!' In a miraculous four-day process, God healed the boy totally.

After this God began to open doors for me to preach in different churches. In one place, as I ministered in a pentecostal tent-meeting, God miraculously and instantly stopped a storm that hit the tent. This was just one of the ways I saw the hand of God move in power, confirming His Word through signs, wonders and miracles.

Chapter 26

Further Training

The summer of 1981, Britta and I went to Rhema Bible Training Center, in Tulsa, Oklahoma, USA. This Bible School has produced many powerful ministers of the Gospel. An example is Ray McCauley of South Africa. Ray McCauley was runner-up in the Mr Universe bodybuilding contest and a friend of Arnold Schwartzenegger. Ray and his wife Lyndie graduated from Rhema, and upon his return home he started a powerful work that has shaken the nation of South Africa. The Rhema Bible Church of South Africa had over 18,000 members in 1993. Ray McCauley, by his message, and by being the brother he is to me, has had a great influence on my life and ministry.

Another powerful minister of the Gospel is my friend Aage Aleskjaer of Oslo, Norway. Aage and his wife Lillemor went to Rhema, and after graduating, started a church. The church grew very fast. In 1993, his church, the Oslo Christian Center, has 2000 members, a Bible School, and a powerful outreach to street people, prostitutes and drug addicts. A large number of the members in the church are people who have been brought to Jesus through the evangelistic outreach of the church.

Getting to Rhema wasn't easy. Rhema, in those days could not help us with student visas, so we had to get visas some other way. At that time the well known American Congregational Church minister Harald Bredesen was visiting Sweden. He came to Uppsala for ministry and heard of our plight. He called a professor friend at Oral Roberts University, Tulsa. This professor, in turn, spoke to ORU graduate Pastor Billy-Joe Daugherty, pastor of Victory Christian Center in Tulsa, who helped us with our visas.

Harald Bredesen was a tremendous man. He always looked happy, always encouraging and speaking faith into peoples' lives no matter where he was. Love always flowed out of his heart. I remember when he visited our tiny apartment. It was a great privilege for Britta and me to receive a visit from such a famous man of God. We had heard how Harald Bredesen used to dine with royalty and presidents, so we decided to cook him a lunch befitting his status. We had checked and found out prior to his visit that he preferred salads. Britta had put a nice tablecloth on the little table in our tiny kitchenette, and we sat around the table. We had a couple of different dishes and a large salad-bowl of salad. I was awed by Harald Bredesen's presence and summoned forth my very best table manners, British-style, learnt at the cadets' mess at the Pakistan Air Force College. Both Britta and I were very tense and formal.

Everything went fine until the end of the meal, when Harald Bredesen suddenly asked, 'anyone for any more salad?' pointing to the large salad-bowl on the table. Upon hearing that nobody wanted any more, he took the large salad-bowl and proceeded to eat directly out of it! All the tension suddenly left and we all burst out laughing. Harald Bredesen was 'real', and I had learnt one of life's great lessons, to be real, whether among royalty or commoners, be yourself, be free as a child of God!

Five of us from Sweden went to Rhema. We were the first Swedes ever to attend. It was a privilege to sit under the powerful and anointed ministry of a man of God like Kenneth Hagin. Our lives were transformed as we listened to the Word of God and watched the move of the Holy Spirit.

Britta had very good grades. I, on the other hand, had never been very academically inclined, but my dear wife pushed me on and I made good grades in all the subjects!

For Britta and me, Rhema was a year of blessing and transformation. We went with very little money, no promise of financial support, and without advertising our material needs. It was amazing to see how God met our needs and blessed us. During that year at Bible school we could give away more money than we had ever done before, even when we held regular jobs back home in Sweden. God was ever faithful, and remained our Jehovah Jireh, our Provider.

We returned to Sweden and began preaching the Word of God.

Chapter 27

Into the Missions Field

My heart was on fire for Missions. I wanted to reach the nations with the Gospel, desperate and eager to go.

My first Missions trip was to Poland, at that time still a Communist country. I ministered in Catholic groups. Many were saved and healed. I stayed at a pig farm along with two Swedish couples who are close friends of mine. There was no television, hamburger-bars or entertainment. All my spare time was taken up by the worship of the Lord Jesus. We got so full of Jesus, it was glorious.

I was asked to come and pray for a man paralysed from his chest down after a traffic accident. I took the two Swedish brothers with me and we went down to the house where the man was.

As I entered the bedroom, my eyes fell on the man lying on the bed. The accident had taken place just recently. He, a mechanic, a man who had been so physically fit, could not fully grasp the fact that he was now paralysed. He lay there, his face showing utter confusion and fear. His wife stood beside the bed. She had been crying, and her eyes were red and swollen. As I stood there, looking at this picture of human suffering, I realized how little man can do in his own power. I did not know what to say. I just felt so small in myself.

Suddenly I sensed that Jesus was there in our midst, and I heard these words come out of me, 'Brother, fear not, because Jesus loves you, and God will raise you up!' I anointed him with oil in the mighty Name of the Lord Jesus. In two minutes he got out of bed and began to walk, hands uplifted, praising God. Several ribs had been broken, and his chest was swollen as a result. His chest came down to normal size instantaneously. When we saw this, we all went down our knees, worshipping and adoring Jesus. We realized that we had nothing to do with this miracle, it was nobody but Jesus; He was there in that room with us, and He alone was worthy to receive all the glory and praise.

Through this miracle many doors were opened for the Gospel in Poland in 1983.

I kept on returning to minister in Poland. Thousands turned to the Lord Jesus. Multitudes of astounding miracles took place. We saw children who had been born totally paralysed, some all twisted up, healed by the power of God. Many blind people received sight, the deaf heard, cancers and tumours disappeared. God healed all kinds of diseases and infirmities.

I remember a young woman in Warsaw, born with her jawbone all twisted and deformed. Doctors had operated on her, trying to correct her hideous deformity. They had put in metal plates, affixed to the bone by metal screws. She came to one of our meetings, and after God healed her, testified, 'As I stood in the crowd with my eyes closed, and you prayed, I felt the hands of God on my jaw, moving, shaping, forming, for about 30 seconds. When I put my hands to my jaw, it was normal!, perfectly shaped, no more deformed, and the metal plates and screws that I earlier could feel with my fingers as I touched my jaw, were totally gone, disappeared!'

A little girl was brought by her mother to a meeting we had in Pila. The girl was totally crippled, having been born with twisted and deformed legs. The legs were folded inwards at the hips and knees in a squatting position. Her knees were drawn up right under her chin, and had been stiff in that position all her life. She had never stood on those legs, neither had she ever been able to straighten them. Thousands were at the meeting. I did not see the girl or the mother, but Jesus saw them and their faith. All of a sudden, I heard people screaming. I looked. People were crying and screaming as this little girl, let down on the floor by her mother, began to walk for the first time in her whole life! The crowd went wild. Suddenly people began to throw aside their sticks and crutches, the crippled began to walk. There was an outburst of miracles, and scores were healed as the Holy Spirit moved over the crowd. The people were pressing forwards for me to pray for them, and I was being crushed. I then took my coat off and tossed it to someone to pass it through the crowd. The healing power of God was so powerful, that as my coat was being passed around through the crowd, from hand to hand, people were healed as they touched the coat.

The priest of the church testified a year later that for three months after that meeting, miracles continued in a continuous stream. People would come to him and leave their sticks and crutches, testifying to what God had done for them.

These are just two examples of the multitudes of

outstanding miracles that the Lord did in Poland. We saw thousands healed from all kinds of diseases and infirmities.

I found the Catholics to have tremendous reverence for the Cross and the Blood of Jesus. They also have great faith to receive miracles from God. On one occasion 12000 people came to a meeting arranged for me by Interland, a Swedish media company, and Polish National Television. I preached on the Blood of Jesus. Thousands were saved and outstanding miracles took place in large numbers. The TV crew chief wept as God touched and healed her where she stood directing her crew. Polish TV made a 70-minute miracle-packed documentary on this service that they telecast free on prime time. As per their estimate, 17 million viewers watched it the first time, nationwide. So many hundreds called the TV station immediately afterwards that their telephone exchange broke down. The programme was re-telecast twice soon after. Such is the power and impact of what the apostle Paul called *'the glorious gospel'*.

Crusade in Malawi, Africa, 1988

Numbers saved in Nkulumane, Zimbabwe

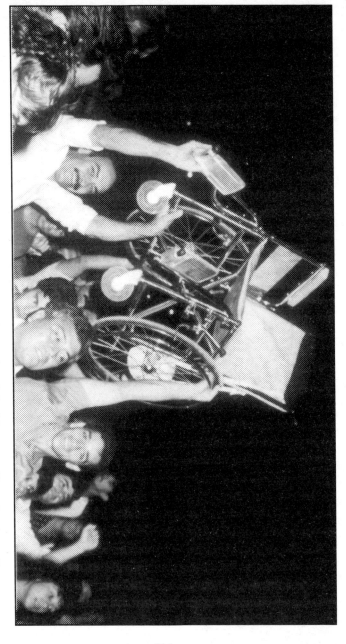

Wheelchair belonging to a woman who was totally paralysed for 16 years – Rosario, Argentina

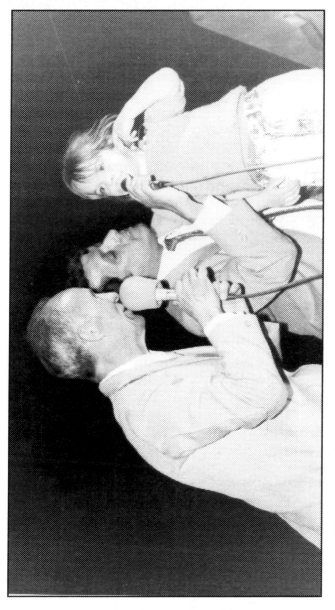

This girl was deaf, but received her hearing at a crusade in Bahia Blanca, Argentina

A tiny girl, totally blind, got her sight in Rosario, Argentina

Chapter 28

To the Ends of the Earth

From humble beginnings, preaching in small groups in Catholic churches in Poland, God has taken us to many nations, on five continents, proclaiming the Gospel of our Lord Jesus Christ to those who have never heard it before. God has moved His mighty hand in many ways.

In Eastern Europe and in Africa we have seen entire towns shaken by the power of God. Many new churches have been established, others have grown and multiplied tremendously. God's ways are so amazing, that we have sometimes even seen great things come out of little situations.

Once, in Malawi, between two major crusades in large cities, I was asked to preach in a little village. About 500 people turned up, and I preached the Gospel standing under a tree. At the end of the meeting, the voice of God came unmistakably. He said, 'There is a woman here who has a mentally-retarded child at home. The child was born with brain damage. Pray for her and I will heal her.'

I said, 'Lord, I don't have the faith for this...'

'I did not ask you if you had the faith,' the Lord replied, 'I have the faith! You just do as I say!'

I called the woman forth, and we prayed over a

cloth that she could lay on her child. She went home, put the child to bed and applied the anointed cloth. The next morning the child woke up perfectly well. God had done it!

The news of this miracle spread like wildfire throughout the district. So many gave their lives to Jesus as result, that five new churches could be started.

God can do anything. At times it takes one single touch of God's power to move a multitude.

We held a crusade in Esikhawini, one of the most violence-torn towns in Kwa-Zulu in the Natal province of South Africa. People were being killed on the streets daily as a result of political violence. My crusade team was also threatened, but we went in, knowing that *'greater is He that is in us than he that is in the world.'* Multitudes gave their lives to to the Lord Jesus, and God did mighty miracles. One outstanding miracle was that of a demon-possessed boy, unable to move, speak, hear or respond in any way. His eyes stared vacantly and expressionlessly into space. He was born normal, but had become like this a few years earlier, because of a witchdoctor's spell. In an instant he was free, totally delivered by God's power.

The really fantastic thing that happened in Esikhawini was that the Gospel stopped the violence. All throughout the week we were there, and for weeks afterwards, not one single killing was reported. The townspeople, for the first time in months, could go outdoors after dark.

In Rosario, Argentina, large multitudes gathered to hear the Gospel. Thousands gave their lives to Jesus every night, and thousands received the baptism with the Holy Ghost and with fire. The Holy

Ghost fell so powerfully that there were those who began to praise God in other tongues in the evening crusade meetings and went on non-stop until the next morning! Large numbers of deaf, deaf-mutes, blind and crippled people were healed, arms and legs grew out up to 20 cms, tumours and cancers disappeared. People who could not walk a step and were confined to wheelchairs, in one case for 16 years, were healed.

Every evening, as I got up to preach, large numbers of demon-possesed people would fall to the ground screaming. They would then be carried to the large 'deliverance tent', where 50 people worked full-time, casting devils out of the people.

Rosario was a headquarters of witchcraft. Literally hundreds were being delivered from the powers of darkness, and even witches and warlocks came to the crusade and were set free.

Some witches, very angry at what was happening, hired a man to kill me. He came to the crusade, and as I preached, he fell on the ground screaming, 'I have been sent to kill Christopher Alam! Tell him to stop preaching!' This man too, was delivered and set free.

For 12 days, God shook Rosario, showing His mighty power to save, heal, and deliver. The very gates of hell were shaken, thousands gave their lives to Jesus, and the devil had a nervous breakdown!

After one of our large crusades in Malawi it was reported that for several days after the end of the crusade, people would bring the sick and the infirm to the field where the crusade had been held. As these people set foot on the ground, they would be healed! How can this be? I believe that the anointed Gospel of Jesus Christ is the most powerful force in the universe. The apostle Paul cried out that the Gospel *'is the power of God ... unto all that believe!'* (Romans 1:16). Wherever this glorious Gospel is preached under the anointing of the Holy Spirit, wherever the precious Blood of Jesus is proclaimed in all its power, that is where the power of God is revealed. It is greater than any preacher. It is so awesome, so great that the human mind cannot even begin to comprehend it!

The omnipotent power of the Holy Spirit, which so filled Peter that it was even in his shadow, is able to permeate even the soil upon which the Gospel is preached. Such is the power of this Glorious Gospel!

It is a fatal mistake to associate God's glory with any man, saying, 'This is because of the anointing and the ministry of so and so.' It is true that God uses man, but what would man be without Jesus? Without Jesus, even the very best of us is nothing.

> *'But we have this treasure in earthen vessels, that the excellency of the power of may be of God, and not of us.'* (2 Corinthians 4:7)

It is not a question of whether the vessel is of gold or silver, but it is a matter of what is in the vessel. When Jesus rode to Jerusalem on a donkey, what mattered was not how fine the donkey was, but it was who it was that rode on the donkey!

In my case, I surely know this, that He does not use me because of who I am, but in spite of who I am!

Without Jesus we are all big zeroes. This has nothing to do with evangelists! This is the power of this glorious Gospel of Jesus Christ the Son of God, and wherever the Gospel is preached, there Jesus is, and shows His power and compassion as He did when he walked on this earth 2000 years ago.

Chapter 29

Reunited at Last

I was born a Muslim, having no knowledge at all of Jesus, the Son of God, and Saviour of all mankind. I was saved from a life filled with much sin, hurt, fear and hate. For seven years my father refused to reply to my letters. He just tore them up. He told everybody that I was dead.

A brother minister visited him on a trip to Bangladesh, where my father had moved to. He told him about my new and firstborn son Immanuel, his first grandchild. Somehow the thought of a grandchild softened his heart. He was grandly proud that it was a boy! He did not send me any greetings through my friend, but sent a gift of 500 pounds sterling to Immanuel!

In 1984 I flew down to him, and stood outside the gates of his house. I rang the bell. A servant came and answered. I asked to see my father. He came. He was older and his hair was white. He stooped ever so slightly, but still had his military bearing. We looked at each other for a few moments then, without a word, we fell into each other's arms and wept. It was a time of healing and restoration.

My stepmother expressed regrets for the past without apologising directly, because that culture does not allow the older to apologise to the younger. Yet, I saw her desire to be reconciled. She cooked my favourite meal of lobster curry. My father treated me like a prince. What amazed me though, was that he very proudly introduced me to his friends as, 'My eldest son, he is a priest in the church in Sweden!' All his friends had believed thus far that I had died seven years earlier! God fully restored my relationship with my father and my stepmother.

I was full of hate, and did not know how to receive love or give love. Today, I love people. I am full of love,

> *'For the Love of God is shed abroad in our hearts by the Holy Ghost which is given unto us.'*
> (Romans 5:5)

I, as a Muslim, hated Jews, today I love the Jews. Through faith in Jesus Christ I also am a seed of Abraham.

As a Pakistani, I hated Indians. Today I love Indians, and have held many Gospel Crusades in India. I have many Indian friends I love dearly.

I once was an outcast, but now I belong to God's wonderful family. I have many brothers and sisters who love me, pray for my family, support us, and show their love in many ways.

Chapter 30

Looking Back...

I stand amazed at the goodness of God. Today, when I think of my past, it seems as though I am thinking about someone else! Jesus is a life changer! In my 22 years as a Muslim I never received a single answer to prayer. Allah never spoke to me, nor did I ever feel his presence in my life. Coming to Jesus changed everything. A distant God who I never knew, the Father of the Lord Jesus Christ, received and embraced me. He became my Father, and I His child. Today I hear the voice of God and know His presence. He is close to me, my heavenly Father. I am His very own child.

He not only saved me and carried me to victory through persecution, He also healed me, baptized me with the Holy Ghost and with fire, and thrust me into the harvest. I have seen cities shaken by the Gospel, the lame walk, the blind see, the deaf hear, the mute speak, twisted and deformed bodies healed by the touch of Jesus; but absolutely the greatest miracle is watching God take a sinner and turn him into a child of God, cleansing him inside and out! Gone are the rags of sin and misery. God clothes us in sparkling white robes of Righteouness.

Some may say, 'O brother, you suffered so much

for the Gospel, it cost you so much..!' To them I would say this, that the real sacrifice and price paid was that which Jesus paid in order to redeem us from our sins and diseases. Oh those tears and bloody sweat at Gethsemane; the lashes at the whipping post; that cruel crown of thorns; the mocking, spitting, and blows of the Roman soldiers; and finally, the pain, the loneliness, the shedding of the precious Blood, and His death upon the Cross at Calvary. Just because of His love for sinners.

Any sacrifice that any of us may ever be called to make, pales in comparison with what it cost Him to purchase our redemption. It is like holding a candle to the sun.

Paul cried out, and I join my cry to his,

> *'But God forbid that I should glory, save in the cross of our Lord Jesus Christ, by whom the world is crucified unto me, and I unto the world!'*
> (Galatians 6:14)

We would be fools to glory in ourselves, or in what we believe that we have done.

There were and are, many others much better than I, but God reached down and saved me and called me because of His own grace and purpose. I cannot yet fully comprehend the fullness of His love and power, but this I know, that he surely has been good to me!

Let this testimony be for the glory of God, to Him alone, who is worthy to receive glory, honour and praise for all that He has done!

> *'For God so loved the world, that He gave His only begotten Son, that whosoever believeth in*

Him should not perish but have everlasting life. For God sent not His Son into the world to condemn the world; but that the world through Him might be saved.' (John 3:16–17)

Chapter 30

Looking Ahead...

I am now part of God's mighty army of evangelists that is shaking this earth through the preaching the Gospel of the Lord Jesus. We are pushing ahead with Gospel Crusades in Africa and ex-communist Eastern Europe.

Since we started this ministry, we have seen a large number of churches born as a result of our work worldwide. Many established churches have grown through our crusades and ministers' seminars. In some places, God has shaken entire towns with the power of the Gospel of Jesus.

I am privileged and blessed to have a wonderful family, and a team of anointed co-labourers. They are precious people, and we stand together for Jesus. They are working hard, laying down their lives for the Gospel. Time is short and Jesus is coming soon. The harvest is plentiful, but the labourers are few. We have preached the Gospel to millions, yet millions are still unreached.

I believe that God wants to bless us with all good things, both spiritually and materially. The Bible says, *'All things are ours!'*, yet the Bible also talks about sacrifice, self-denial, and laying down our lives for the Gospel of the Lord Jesus. God may, at times, call us to sacrifice or lay down certain 'good' things so that others may have that which is exceedingly better and most excellent – the knowledge of Jesus Christ the Saviour and Lord. We do not know how much time we have left to finish the task the Lord has entrusted us with. The Great Commission to preach the Gospel to every creature. Yes, the task is great, but the power and grace given to us are far greater and exceedingly more abundant. There is salvation, healing, deliverance, in rich abundance, for all that believe!

What will you do with your life? Will you say '**Yes!**' to the call of God, and follow?

God will anoint you with the Holy Ghost and with fire!

Your heart is the altar of God. In Leviticus 6:13 is written the commandment of the Lord,

> *'The fire shall ever be burning upon the altar; it shall never go out.'*

Say '**Yes Lord!**' to Jesus, and let Him send His fire to fall upon you, setting you ablaze for His kingdom and His glory. Let us arise together and win this world for Jesus!

> *'Put ye in the sickle, for the harvest is ripe ... !'*
> (Joel 3:13)

Jesus is coming soon! Are you ready?

An Invitation to You

If this book has touched your heart and you want to receive Jesus Christ as your Lord and Saviour, please pray this simple prayer.

'Father God, I come to you in the Name of your Son Jesus Christ.
Lord Jesus, I thank you for shedding your precious blood upon the Cross for me.
I believe that you died for me and rose again.
I believe that you are alive today.
Jesus, I give you all my sin. Wash me in your precious Blood. Wash me white as snow.
Come into my heart right now and be the Lord of my life.
Amen.'

If you have prayed this prayer, I advise you to contact the closest Bible-believing church. Tell them of your decision to follow Jesus. They will be glad to help and guide you in any way you may require.

Don't forget the four steps to victory!
1. Read your Bible.
2. Pray; talk to God.
3. Fellowship with strong Christians and go to a good church.
4. Tell others about what Jesus has done in your life.